GET

"!"

OPINIONATED

A Progressive's Guide
to Finding Your Voice
(and Taking a Little Action)

AMANDA MARCOTTE

SEAL PRESS

GET OPINIONATED
A Progressive's Guide to Finding Your Voice (and Taking a Little Action)

Copyright © 2010 by Amanda Marcotte

Published by
Seal Press
A Member of Perseus Books Group
1700 Fourth Street
Berkeley, California 94710

Library of Congress Cataloging-in-Publication Data

Marcotte, Amanda.
  Get opinionated : a progressive's guide to finding your voice (and taking a little action) / by Amanda Marcotte.
      p. cm.
   ISBN 978-1-58005-302-0
   1. Women—Political activity—United States—Handbooks, manuals, etc.
   2. Women political activists—United States—Handbooks, manuals, etc.
   I. Title.
   HQ1236.5.U6M373 2010
   322.4082'0973—dc22
                                    2009025400

9 8 7 6 5 4 3 2 1

Cover and interior design by Domini Dragoone
Printed in the United States of America by Edwards Brothers
Distributed by Publishers Group West

CONTENTS

CHAPTER ONE

YOU DON'T HAVE TO BE A STINKY HIPPIE

- The Dirty Little Secret of Living Green: *It's Fun*
- The Other Dirty Little Secret of Living Green: *It's Not Enough*
- Atkins: An Environmental Disaster
- Grow Your Own Way: Gardening for Food, Gardening against Global Warming

ACTION: "Reduce, Reuse, Recycle" Reaches Its Sexiness Peak

CHAPTER TWO

READ A BOOK, OR AT LEAST A BLOG:
The Pitfalls of Learning

- "Fair and Balanced," My Ass
- Knowing Who to Vote for Shouldn't Require Sixty Hours of Research
- Who Says a Liberal Can't Get the Ratings?

ACTION: Don't Turn the TV Off—Turn Yourself On

INTRODUCTION

Eight years of George W. Bush devastated the country, but American liberalism, which had been declared all but dead after decades of demonization by the right-wing noise machine, saw a renaissance during his presidency. Prior to the Bush years, liberals had been a scattershot, incoherent group who didn't necessarily feel we had much in common. To make it worse, "liberal" had become a dirty word that most people wouldn't cop to, and many instead tried on the weasel word "progressive." Union supporters often came to blows with environmentalists, feminism and anti-racism relied increasingly on academic institutions instead of on-the-ground politics to define them, and, let's face it, Bill Clinton, with his trade agreements and deregulation schemes (which helped destroy the economy a decade later—thanks, Bill!), made even the few people left who were willing to call themselves liberals turn on the Democrats. It was hard for many people to even care when Al Gore saw the election blatantly stolen from him, with the assistance of the Supreme Court.

Few things equal the unifying, clarifying power of hate, however. Bush didn't do us any favors, but he did become the perfect villain to bring these disparate people together under a common banner. Since we live in a cynical age, my description of the situation sounds, unfortunately, a bit like I'm mocking the concept of Bush the Supervillain, but rest assured, I'm not. Without a trace of irony, the man really did offer himself up as the sort of person you love to hate—right before you feel bad about taking even sick pleasure in hating him, because doing so clouds the purity of your righteous hate. You couldn't ask for a better person to bring unity to the left, because no matter what flavor of liberal you were, Bush would chew you up as eagerly as he did the other flavors.

Bush swung at peaceniks, atheists, freedom lovers, human-rights activists, feminists, labor, environmentalists, and even apolitical people who preferred to keep their Social Security, all with the same giant baseball bat. It wasn't just that he didn't play favorites when it came to liberal issues he pissed all over; it was about the gushing amounts of piss he poured over those issues. Believe me, as someone who spent much of my effort focusing on reproductive rights, I kept having to fill up the sink with cold water and dunk my head in it, just to make sure that I wasn't making it up when the Bush administration did something aggressively misogynist. It was never enough to merely appoint anti-choice judges, though the Christian right really didn't need more to win their votes. The Bush administration made a point of skipping way to the right of people's worst expectations, reaching a height of right-wing-nut insanity when Bush-appointed FDA officials refused to authorize over-the-counter emergency contraception because they feared that it would kick-start teenage sex cults.

I can't speak with the same depth of authority on other subjects as I can on that one, but my discussions with activists from other realms indicate that Bush shot past people's disrespect and began earning their open contempt in almost every issue area imaginable, though I don't think Americans really understood the levels of that contempt until Bush blew off thousands of them when New Orleans nearly washed away in a hurricane.

Bunker mentality turned many people into angry ranters, but when everyone's stuck in the same bunker, they realize they have cramped muscles and a desire to see light in common, and that can bring people together. Eight years of Bush turned "liberal" into an identity, and liberals became a community. It had political benefits, and frankly, it had social benefits, as you could wander into any random party in your social stratosphere and assume everyone else was on the same political page as you. For political nerds, the ability to talk about politics at parties provided a small comfort during those dark Bush years. Calling yourself a liberal without flinching went from being an act of bravery to being mundane. After all, the defining feature of a liberal was wanting Bush's ass out of office, right? That made liberalism the mainstream.

Barack Obama was assumed to be a unifying figure that brought liberals out of the closet and united the country, but a more accurate assessment would be that he ran a campaign that read the national mood and fed it back to us as his own message. Liberals had already come out, and the country had already decided to kick Republicans out. We'd created the space for the candidate, and he just stepped into the role with aplomb. That doesn't detract from the sheer joy and unity Obama supporters felt the night of the 2008 presidential election, but even as I joined in the jubilant celebration, I felt people were rejoicing more about what we had done by electing Obama than about what he had done by winning. We'd decided we were liberals. We'd come out as liberals. We'd joined up with others and elected a president. And we were going to party.

No one can take that from us. But now, as we finally finish up our last cup of coffee and emerge from our Bush hangover, the question we have to ask ourselves is, "Yes, I'm a liberal, but what does that even mean?"

In the memories of most politically minded people, liberal has gone through only two phases: dirty word and Bush hater. It's been defined only as a negative, so, now that we're looking at a Democratic majority, it would be helpful if we could define what "liberal" is, instead of what it's not. This sounds easier than it is; I've been a political blogger and writer for over five years now, and the Obama victory made me realize how many of my political opinions are about what I don't believe instead of what I do. Now that we've got power, we'd better start getting opinionated.

I don't think the opposition suffers from this problem, which just makes the situation more urgent. Conservatives often have a very good definition of what they believe and what they expect to come out of it. They do often have the benefit of the past to look to, and every flavor of conservatism out there harkens back to a time that conservatives think of as the "golden era," despite the objective fact that it sucked shit for the majority of people. Conservatives long for colonialism, the days before women's rights, and a time when black people had no other choice but to work low-wage jobs with no hope of improving their station. A time when Christianity was promoted in the schools, men could rule over their families with an iron fist, and you could pretend that you were invading another country and taking its resources for its own good and no one would question the audacity of that. It's an unpleasant vision, but it's a very clear, well-documented one. While many Republican voters are just bundles of badly articulated racism, sexism, and aimless rage, their actual writers, campaigners, and activists have a very clear vision of what they believe and what they wish to accomplish.

That clarity results in votes and power. Americans especially respect people who know what they want and what it will take to get it, and they'll respect it even if they don't agree with it at all. For decades, Democratic partisans would wring their hands and wonder how the Republicans did it, over and over—put up a politician like George Bush, with half the wits, intelligence, and even charm of someone like John Kerry or Al Gore, and win anyway. We assumed they had some political masterminds and some magic formula for distracting people from reality and turning them to fantasy. We built up a halfwit like Karl Rove to be some kind of criminal mastermind, even though his main talent seems to be excessive assholery, coupled with an outrageous and undeserved sense of self-esteem.

There was no mastermind, no magic formula, no brilliance at all. What conservatives have had for a long time that liberals haven't is a clarity of purpose. They have strong opinions about what they want the country to look like, and strong ideas about how to get there. Liberals have had a hodgepodge of political correctness, infighting, and an unwillingness to even label ourselves liberals. But as soon as we had the clarity of purpose that hating Bush brought us, we were able to pull out some victories.

But we can't lean on Bush hatred anymore. Nor can we scatter to the winds and let a bunch of stubborn right-wing nuts take the country over yet again. In an attempt to push the dialogue forward, I wrote this book to give some shape and definition to major issues that liberals should embrace as their own, no matter what angle they come from.

To be clear, in writing this I'm not trying to lay down dogma or say there's only one correct liberal opinion on this issue or that. One strength of being on the left instead of the right is that you don't have to put up with that law-laying, near religious approach to opinion forming. We should be proud that we don't echo the same meaningless platitudes to each other and consider that discourse. In that spirit, I offer more my own personal vision of liberalism than a prescription for others. I hope to provoke more than dictate, and ideally, readers will go on from this book to engage in other forms of media—not just other books and magazines, but blogs and other websites where they can practice their opinionating skills.

What I do want you to take away from this book is not liberal dogma, but a belief that these various issues are intertwined, and that someone who comes to liberalism for issue X will do well to care about issues Y and Z as well. Don't let people pigeonhole you! You may start off as a feminist, but there's no reason not to add "environmentalist" to your list of interests. Liberal economics, anti-racism, secularism, and support for science—these seemingly disparate issues have more in common than they would seem to have at first blush, and they work together in interesting ways.

Liberals have allowed our various issues to get siloed off from each other. The word "values" alone has much to do with this—the mainstream media considers conservatives those who have a unifying values system, and liberals just a bunch of single-issue types who have to hang together or we'll hang separately. But we do have values. Often, they're so basic that they don't even get labeled as values so much as, "Well, duh." We value equality, freedom, community, and health. These liberal values are so ingrained that conservatives have to pretend to value them to smuggle hostile arguments—for instance, they want to roll back anti-racism gains like affirmative action in the name of equality. Don't let this sort of disingenuous fuckwittery distract you—you have values that hold your various opinions together, and the static from conservatives trying to confuse the issue has to be tuned out.

My main hope with this book is that you'll read it, get opinionated, and start speaking up. And don't worry about the cacophony that results when we add so many more voices to the mix. Cacophony can confuse, but mostly it creates volume. Only by getting out there and expressing our opinions can we even get noticed by or influence our leaders.

Again, the right figured this out a long time ago. That's why there's a right-wing noise machine, even though the vast majority of stuff it puts out is nonsensical, paranoid, and downright hateful. It doesn't matter. By making noise, the machine demonstrates that the right has numbers (and hell, it makes those numbers look even higher than they are, it's so noisy), and that alone makes the right formidable.

We can be noisy without being crippled by stupidity, paranoia, racism, and an inexplicable loathing of rumpled academics. We can easily best these bastards, who set the bar incredibly low. Loud liberals' victory in the war of words against loud conservatives should, if it's done with the proper vim and vigor, be a matter of someone wearing a neat Armani suit beating someone in neon-colored MC Hammer pants in a fashion contest. It's just a matter of putting yourself out there. So get to it! Wait, no—read my book first, and then get to it!

A TOUR THROUGH
Your Various Political Types

Sadly, having good liberal political opinions isn't enough, even if you back them up with sound facts and logic. Ours is a highly diverse social species, and politics is as much a game of finessing and understanding personalities and roles as it is one of understanding facts and arguments. With that in mind, here's a tour of some of the major types of people you'll meet in the hairy world of arguing politics.

SOCIALLY CONSERVATIVE PATRIARCHS

After the reign of George W. Bush, with all his fundamentalist support and fundamentalist-scripted policy, the socially conservative patriarch became *the* face of conservatism in America. More James Dobson than Rush Limbaugh (though members of the Limbaugh wing wisely pretend to endorse conservative religious values before they go do some drugs and foist themselves on underage prostitutes), the socially conservative patriarchs heard the anguished cries of men around the country whose wives were clueing in to feminism and wanting help doing the dishes and the right to quit faking orgasms. The patriarchs' answer to these men's woes? Jesus. Jesus would make it all better. Jesus would tell your wife to submit. Jesus would tell those gays to get back in the closet. Jesus would make you feel like you were all man, even if you liked wearing chinos and *Seinfeld*'s humor went over your head.

"Family" is the word that gets this type excited, and hopefully in a totally nonsexual way, though the amount of time and attention socially conservative patriarchs expend on monitoring the status of their teenage daughters' hymens often causes outsiders to think that may not always be the case. Worse, if a Republican politician is caught up in a sex scandal, he's almost surely going to be the sort who acts in public like he sleeps with a bible under his pillow. What David Vitter (paid women to have sex with him while he wore diapers), Larry Craig (arrested for attempting to have anonymous gay sex in an airport bathroom), and Mark Foley (caught chasing underage congressional pages in hopes the boys would have sex with him) have in common, besides getting turned out by coloring outside the sexual lines, is that they are all bible-thumping, family-values conservatives.

Though you may sense that socially conservative patriarchs are the type you should never be alone in a room with, you can also identify their kind by their forced congeniality, their aggressive unwillingness to look palatable, and their strong streak of prissiness, which probably explains why they're so worried someone will think they're anything less than all man. They talk a lot about muscular Christianity but enjoy breaking into tears when discussing how much the anti-abortion, anti-gay Jesus means to them. And while some may think they can still get away with preaching about how that rock 'n' roll is making all the young girls loose, most have updated their shtick so they're panicking about how rappers are taking perfectly fine girls with intact hymens and turning them into hussies.

Their version of utopia: Splitting their time between having their sons look at them worshipfully, having their daughters tell them graphically what they *won't* be doing sexually until Daddy signs off on the wedding and makes it okay, and going to religious and professional occasions where they can huff and puff about how important they are. All such occasions should be accompanied by wife-supplied food that is carefully monitored to make sure it never gets too healthy or includes too many spices that remind anyone of "ethnic" cuisine.

SOCIALLY CONSERVATIVE SISTER PUNISHERS

Sarah Palin's ascent to the vice-presidential slot of the Republican ticket in 2008 marked a new peak in sister punishers' journey from being the ladies' auxiliary of conservatism to being a major force driving the Republican party. Anti-feminists want us little ladies to know that we're not important, yet shooting down feminism has become such a widespread right-wing activity that the cute little ladies' group of official anti-feminist voices has become a major player. If it inspires that much resistance, feminism must be important indeed.

Sister punishers play many roles—they get to speak out against taxes, immigration, and the evils of the liberal elite—but they exist mostly to prove to the world that the misogynist, anti-feminist engine that runs so much modern conservatism can't be all that bad when it's got so many hot bitches onboard. In that spirit, what sister punishers say often matters less than how they look and how good a job they do at convincing the audience that they've barely touched cock (but they'd totally touch yours).

Conservatives promote a lot of stereotypes about feminists that don't hold up: that feminists are ugly, hate men, are slutty or sexually frigid, don't shave, are lesbians, and will fuck every man they meet so they can have more abortions. Some feminists fit some of these stereotypes and others fit none, but no one can, for reasons of logic, fit all of them. Sister punishers set out to prove these stereotypes by not fitting them. The logic is that if anti-feminists are not sweaty, hairy, frigid sluts, then feminists must be. Therefore, sister punishers must be sexually warm but also inexperienced, gorgeous and fuckable but modest. Sarah Palin grabbed the national imagination because she could maintain the illusion, for entire minutes at a time, that this balance was possible.

Being a sister punisher means practicing the most outlandish hypocrisy: Sister punishers hit the road to tell women to get back to the kitchen. They preach abstinence until marriage but give birth to full-term babies seven months after their wedding (like Sarah Palin did). They throw bombs about slutty, single women while being Ann Coulter. They claim, as Gayle Haggard did, that wifely submission brings endless joy and then wear their martyrdom on their sleeves, as she did when her minister husband, Ted Haggard, was revealed to be visiting male prostitutes. They sniff about the impropriety of how women dress these days but then shrug it off when men commit the greater offense of rape. They pride themselves on their intelligence while writing off women as the stupider sex.

Their version of utopia: Since I can't write about this breed without referring to Margaret Atwood's classic sci-fi novel *The Handmaid's Tale,* I have to point out that Atwood made the clever observation that sister punishers would be thrust into hell if they achieved their goals. In a world where women's place really was in the home, they would all retreat to their houses and leave the road, the TV, and the op-ed pages. So the world we have, where women are permitted some amount of freedom but blatant misogyny still has a place in the public discourse, is in fact sister punishers' utopia. Lucky them.

MANIC PIXIE DREAM GIRL LIBERAL CHICKS

Nathan Rabin, of the Onion AV Club, defined the manic pixie dream girl as a movie-character type that springs more from male fantasies than from real life. To quote Rabin: "The manic pixie dream girl exists solely in the fevered imaginations of sensitive writer-directors to teach broodingly soulful young men to embrace life and its infinite mysteries and adventures." She doesn't stick around long—she moves on (or, preferably, dies) before you really get to know her.

She has a counterpart in real life: the compassionate liberal woman who haunts the dreams of young men who hit peace rallies in hopes of scoring. She eschews shoes, slacks, and feminism as energy-sucks that interfere with her being a ray of pure sex and understanding. She's against war, meat eating, and bad vibes. She's free of sexual hang-ups and hopes to home-school a brood of barefoot children one day. She won't resist you, even if you're talking down to her—she's too busy dancing in a field of poppies. She even manages to make the combination of white-girl dreads and a Brazilian bikini wax make sense.

Manic pixie dream girl liberal chicks have one major drawback that interferes with their ability to be perfectly unthreatening fantasy girls, though: You have to compete with PETA for their affection. If PETA gets its hooks into your dream girl, you can expect that she'll not only convert to a vegan diet and get preachy on you but also start stripping down in public at animal-rights protests. If you try to stop this behavior, you'll come across as someone who wants to murder kittens.

Their version of utopia: A communal living arrangement in which none of their roommates screws up by using animal-unfriendly products. Soft carpets all over the world, and no one stepping on their feet. Also, a world where nonscratchy and effective hemp condoms exist.

LESS FUN FEMINIST LIBERAL CHICKS

It's not that less fun feminists all resist dressing in a way that might be attractive to the male eye; it's just that feminists balance that desire with wishing to be taken seriously, being comfortable, and maintaining an acute sense of dignity that manic pixie dream girls don't have. Of course, plenty of feminists have no reason to dress according to male desires, because they aren't into men or because they can't reconcile it with their politics. Those who do feel the tug of male approval spend an inordinate amount of time wavering between political correctness and beauty standards, but even a feminist who caves in to the Brazilian wax will never, ever dance in a field of poppies. Or gaze at you adoringly when you say, "Now that I think about it, U2 *is* overrated."

Feminists really don't like sexism, so if you're a man who benefits from being sexist, this can make you routinely uncomfortable. Watching Bangbus porn, constricting your opinions on women you meet to whether or not you'd fuck them, and monopolizing the conversation are all behaviors that less fun feminist chicks will question a dude about. These women won't have a standard sexual MO that makes them easy to figure out—some are monogamous, some are less so, some are lesbians, some are straight, and some won't tell you what they are, because it's none of your business unless you yourself are sexually involved with them.

Feminists are less fun for easily threatened men, but don't let the stereotypes about their lack of a sense of humor chase you off. In fact, feminists have infiltrated the comedy business, sneaking up on you and making you laugh before you know it: They smuggle themselves in under your radar in shapes labeled Margaret Cho, Tina Fey, Wanda Sykes, and Amy Poehler. Only fellow feminists, recognizing that these sorts of high achievers are inevitable in any industry, could have seen this coming.

Less fun feminists look you in the eye and don't giggle helplessly. They're easily irritated when their intelligence is underestimated. They give to NARAL and roll their eyes when they hear someone equivocate on abortion rights. When they reach middle age, they think it's funny to tell people that middle-aged women are invisible, and that that's freeing. They've heard about homeschooling but find affordable daycare (or avoiding children altogether) closer to their tastes. They love to dance with their shoes on, talk politics with their girlfriends, and drink gin and tonics. They think *The View* is stupid but will praise it for taking on politics anyway.

Their version of utopia: Having a female president, free birth control, and no one talking down to them at work, and coming home to find that their male partner has done exactly 50 percent of the housework without being nagged about it. Frequent sex that's not over until they've had half a dozen orgasms.

LIBERAL DUDES

The kind, but not necessarily mild-mannered, liberal dude is a common enough type, but *not* the kind that feminists are thinking of when they complain about "liberal men." These are well-meaning liberal guys who, being good liberals, take women's word for it when women make feminist statements. They may even label themselves "feminist"—though only when asked, because all men everywhere find the idea of a male feminist strange and off-putting.

Anti-war but also obstinately against the people who carry FREE MUMIA signs to protests, pro-labor but uneducated about union politics—these guys were proud to have OBAMA signs in their front yards during the primary and reluctant to take them down in the days after the election, wanting the moment to last a little bit longer. They respond to right-wing men by declaring that they don't need guns to prove that they're men, and they try to do half the housework (and often succeed in doing up to a third of it). They fully intend, if they ever get a woman pregnant, to state, "It's your choice," and to never waver from that position. They don't want their wives to take their names, and they get whipped up when someone dismisses the importance of gays' right to marry. They constitute a solid percentage of liberal bloggers overall but dominate the ranks of the highest traffic liberal bloggers.

They're big on public transportation and universal health care. They declared that Hillary Clinton was a perfectly acceptable second choice during the primaries, though they started to get angry at the women who clung to Clinton, believing until the bitter end that she could win. They consider themselves anti-capitalist but love Apple products and play the stock market, and 85 percent of them have jobs in the private sector (law, computers, and marketing are favorites), because they're men and they're smart and they can make a lot of money.

Al Gore is indebted mostly to these guys for his post-2000 ascendancy as a national environmentalist hero. Once he was safely tucked away from the nefarious influence of Joe Lieberman and the neoliberals who polluted the Clinton administration, Gore was free to seem like a rare good man in the dirty world of politics, and astute liberal men (and commonsensical feminist liberal women) ate it up, actually spending an evening watching Gore's documentary about global warming, which most people would consider a weird way to entertain yourself.

These guys marry the less fun feminist chicks, whereupon they turn into urban liberal couples (see below).

Their version of utopia: A world much like ours, but with cleaner technology, more TV shows like *The Wire,* time to perfect their skills as gourmet chefs, and a Democratic party that sucks a little less at both policy and politics. Also national health care.

LIBERAL DUDES WHO SCOLD
FEMINISTS ABOUT "IMPORTANT" ISSUES

These guys have felt like they know everything about politics since the day they read *The Autobiography of Malcolm X* their freshman year of college. They wear long hair and totally have a hard-on for manic pixie dream girls, but they all too often end up in bed with the less fun feminists, whom they then end up dogging like a motherfucker about how feminism is a symptom of class privilege. If they don't have feminist girlfriends to dog about this stuff, they dog feminists online or at political meetings or in coffeehouses. There's always something that's more important than women's rights: the war, the economy, the eternal class struggle, the race issue. Not that feminism is wrong, but if we correct all these other problems, women's problems will correct themselves. Meanwhile, the stereotypical ambitious feminist who would rather have decent daycare than homeschool her kids is another symptom of our sick world.

Going to a scolding liberal dude's house can be an adventure. Remember: You have to take your shoes off when you come in, because he finds that he saves more electricity (and effort) if he has to vacuum less. His dog, however, is free to roam around the house after being outside without having his paws cleaned. Avoid the papasan chair purchased at a garage sale, and if you sleep over, know that you're sleeping on a single mattress on the floor. Don't ask what the Chinese symbols in the paintings on liberal dude's wall mean; even if he thinks he knows, he probably doesn't. He may or may not drink alcohol, but he will definitely know how to get the good weed. If you want to know who's been waving that FREE MUMIA sign at the anti-war protests, you have your culprit.

If you want to get on this guy's good side, don't talk about reproductive-rights activism or the struggle for same-sex marriage—you're just asking for a lecture on priorities. Ask him about Saul Alinsky, or about how he thinks the United States could go about unilaterally ceasing and reversing our imperialist policies. Just don't ask him whether he thinks the left should embrace gradual progress or flirt with revolution if you want him to shut up any time in the next four hours.

These dudes aren't unilaterally opposed to all feminist activism—if abortion were made illegal and they were needed to help run a radical underground-abortion service, they'd jump at the opportunity. But boring, middle-of-the-road issues, like equal pay for equal work, make their eyelids drift closed.

Their version of utopia: Making a livelihood as a folk musician, having a manic pixie dream girl come over twice a week to get them off and leave, and attending a Phish reunion with the possibility of securing lifetime financial aid toward the important mission of following the band forever.

COLLEGE REPUBLICANS

Of all conservative affectations, the pose of victimhood makes the least sense to liberals. Where do people who never have to prove their intelligence (and thank god that's the case for most of them, because they'd fail) or merit, whose race, sex, and class privilege guarantee good jobs, big houses, and never having to face people who reveal that they aren't interesting or funny, get off saying they're victims? Angry White Male syndrome irritates on a number of levels, but the false mantle of victimhood irritates the most. What could college Republicans want that they're missing?

Spend some time around college Republicans—i.e., right-wing resenters in their embryonic stage—and you'll get a better idea of how to answer that question. The young, privileged white men who can expect a future of golf clubs and obedient wives, and whose sexist jokes send them into uncontrollable twitters, spend their college years adrift in a sea of people who feel no need to hide their opinion that the college Republicans are megawatt douchebags. And that blow to their ego will last them the rest of their lives, no matter how many acres of golf course they put between themselves and the sexually satisfied hippies who laugh at them.

The psychology of college Republicans, and why they seethe now and will for the rest of their lives, made complete sense to me one day as I strolled across the campus of the University of Texas at Austin on an otherwise innocuous day. A group of khaki-clad, roly-poly young white men sat in folding chairs in front of the library with a giant boom box blasting the irritating voice of Rush Limbaugh across the yard; their display came complete with a sign that read: Because We Have a Right.

So much became apparent right then: This group of young men was shut off, due to their obnoxious personalities, from the pleasures of college life surrounding them. Leggy young women would not fuck them, and guys with cool record collections would not offer to smoke them out. They would never have that moment of genuinely feeling like they were learning something profound during their studies. Late-night giggle sessions at diners, awesome rock shows, and making out with that person they'd been eyeballing for months at a party—all wonderful experiences, all shut off from them. No matter how many golf clubs and Hummers their future held, they would never be able to buy cool, and they knew it. So they thought they'd torture the people they'd never be by making us listen to five minutes of Rush Limbaugh and experiencing, if just for a moment, the hell that was being them.

Taken from that point of view, a softhearted liberal might almost feel sorry for these wankers. If you feel that sympathy moving your heart, remember that these people think that bombing foreign countries will help quiet the resentments that eat at their soul. Don't pity them. They had the choice to shut off the talk radio, buy a David Bowie album and some blue jeans, and stop sucking. They just didn't take it.

Their version of utopia: The idea of a world that provides actual joy based in real experiences eludes college Republicans. The closest they can come to a utopian paradise is a world where they have a bunch of liberals, feminists, and anyone who seems to be mildly decent and/or relaxed tied up in a room with duct tape over their mouths. Then the college Republicans could stage plays about the evils of immigration, abortion, and taxes, so they could feed off their victims' nervous breakdowns. And, of course, those victims deserve it—they shouldn't have thought they were so cool in the first place.

COUNTRY CLUB REPUBLICANS

Liberals contemplating the dilemma of country club Republicans often swing between pity and schadenfreude these days. After all, country clubbers spent a lot of time and money cozying up to the bible thumpers and conspiracy-theory crazies to get votes for their party: the party of tax breaks for the rich and relentless opposition to the minimum wage. They probably never intended to give those people any power—just to get their votes, cash their checks, and then hit the links. A perfect plan, except that the crazies took over the party, and now it's less golf and more trying to make a case that Barack Obama's funny name means he can't have been born in the United States, right?

Country club Republicans are simple people. They want to play golf and read George Will's rants about baseball, ungrateful kids, and how global warming is something stupid hippies made up because hippies are motivated by pure evil (you can tell by their haircuts). They enjoyed sharing a party with the bible-thumping nutters and black-helicopter types because the fact that they could just gather these people around to vote for tax cuts for themselves reinforced how superior they were to everyone else.

But when the head country clubber of the United States, Dick Cheney, had to hide behind George W. Bush to get into office, perhaps the clubbers should have realized the tide was turning. True, Bush was from the pre-eminent country club family in the country, but he got elected by putting forward a passable impression of a good ol' boy with a bible in one hand and a gun in the other—the sort of impression Cheney couldn't pull off before he told some kid to get off his lawn and broke his cover. The clubbers gave themselves permission to look the other way by assuming Cheney was the power behind the throne.

And then John McCain, another country club Republican, found himself having to whoop it up and perform like he was more comfortable pounding a bible than he was eating caviar for a crowd of angry right-wingers, and the clubbers realized the gig was up. Regaining control of the party that belongs to them will hopefully turn out to be harder than they could have ever imagined.

Their version of utopia: Business meeting at ten, lunch at noon, links at three. Never having to pay a dime in estate taxes. And it would be nice if scientists created a better breed of poor people, so country clubbers' servants never gave them cause to believe them insubordinate.

URBAN LIBERAL COUPLES

Toyota Priuses, Montessori schools, and the Gap were made for them. They work in law, academia, marketing, or computers and, as such, flock to urban centers where the work is and where Whole Foods, fusion restaurants, and stores with massive wine selections are. They're why NARAL, the ACLU, and gay-marriage organizations do so well with fundraising. Same story with Barack Obama's campaign. They saw themselves in Obama, with his fashionable clothes, smart wife, adorable children, interest in keeping himself healthy, and secret smoking problem. Obama is still a little hip for all his ambitious and hardworking qualities, and that's what every urban liberal wants to be.

This type spans both the baby boomer generation and Generation X, the major difference between them being that the former clings to coolness by retaining its Grateful Dead records and perhaps having a collection of doodads from around the world (often with a Native American focus), while the Gen Xers lean more toward having concert or pop art (always tastefully framed). No matter what their age, they love *The Daily Show* and they love rock music, and most drift from a period of being on top of the newest music to being set in their ways without even realizing it.

They're environmentalists who long for universal health care and good public transportation and shop at farmers' markets, but they're not anti-capitalist, no matter what Rush Limbaugh says. They're downright brand-conscious, in fact, especially when it comes to Apple products. They're the people who got fair-trade coffee into Starbucks, and massage therapists into Microsoft.

Everyone loathes them.

No, really. When right-wing talk-radio hosts rant about the "liberal elite," they mean these folks. Leftists hate them, too, calling them sellouts or worse, and suggest that liberals' tolerance of capitalism may be worse than conservatives' championing thereof. Urban liberals even kind of loathe themselves, or at least are eager to trip over themselves to make fun of themselves, which is why the website Stuff White People Like was such a massive hit. This very section is another flavor of that same type of mockery.

Their version of utopia: One where Republican voters calmed the fuck down, looked over the facts, and started voting like sensible beings, instead of a rabid pack of uneducated reactionaries. Urban liberals don't need much more than that, because, outside of the world of politics, we're talking about a pretty satisfied group of people—or self-satisfied, if you prefer.

RUSH LIMBAUGH IMPOTENTS

Not all fans of Rush Limbaugh—or right-wing talk radio in general—fit into this type, but these people nonetheless comprise the ideal demographic of such radio shows. Some were college Republicans, and some came into politics late in life, but all of the above have a strong love of angry ranting based on hating all people who appear not to hate themselves as much as the impotents hate them. These people get classified as "liberals" and become the prime focus of all the rage that's generated by a personal sense, and possibly literal problem with impotence.

Rush Limbaugh followers are attracted to racism and sexism and general anger, but mostly they just want to find a way to hate people who have stuff they don't have that they think these people don't deserve, but whom they also envy in their bone marrow. This audience eats up stories about the "liberal elite," with their lattes and birth control pills. When you hear a right-wing pundit bashing liberal college professors, he's aiming at this audience, which resents those smarty-pants who think they know everything because they read so much. Ditto for career women, racial minorities who have supposedly benefited from affirmative action, and Hollywood movie stars—all people whose main crime is having luxuries, self-esteem, or personal fulfillment that Limbaugh's target demographic is missing.

Mostly, they don't have a coherent ideology to hang all this resentment and weirdness on, unlike their libertarian or socially conservative brethren. For instance, most of this type will admit to being pro-choice should it come up in private conversation, mostly because they see no point in banning abortion. But should Rush rant about "feminazis" who supposedly love abortion, they'll nod eagerly in agreement. Fuck those bitches, with all their sex that the impotents aren't getting and all those rights they don't deserve (not that the impotents will ever really strike out against them). Same with taxes—they'll rail against those ungrateful welfare recipients with their huge checks, but they couldn't, if pressed, name a single welfare program or suggest a reasonable place to make a cut.

The impotents voted for John McCain, and while they often had half-baked, logical-sounding reasons for it, mostly they were swept into a tidal wave of hate for Barack Obama, due to his thinking he's so smart. His wife, with her nice clothes and intelligence, didn't make their jealousy any less severe.

Interestingly, this group of resentful losers is highly prone to eating up libertarian rhetoric about how Democrats want to redistribute wealth to the less deserving. The only explanation for this tendency is that they also engage in self-fluffing about being heroes from Ayn Rand novels to quiet the self-loathing within them. Indeed, if you see someone reading a Rand novel in public, odds run very high that said person will have unchecked acne, bad taste in clothing, and an inability to hide his desperate lack of sexual experience, yet he believes he can relate to the superhumans of Randian lore.

Of all the visible McCain supporters, Joe the Plumber epitomized this type the best. After he accosted candidate Obama and asked if Obama intended to raise his taxes (the implication being that Joe the Plumber made over $250,000 a year from his personal business after he paid expenses, the only possible way he'd be facing a tax raise), the media discovered that not only did Joe not work for himself or have any chance of making over $250,000 a year, but his name wasn't even Joe and he wasn't a certified plumber.

No matter. In Limbaugh-land, he's both a member of the underappreciated Randian superclass and the sort of person who gets swept up in hating a long litany of people he secretly suspects are smarter than he is, get laid more than he does, and don't hate themselves as much as he does. He doesn't need to understand policy or politics when he's got all that.

Of course, the biggest impotent of all is and has always been Rush Limbaugh: ex-husband to many, and boil on the butt of humanity.

Their version of utopia: A big group of sexy young women, college professors, black yuppies, the Clintons and their friends, urban latte drinkers, people who own Priuses, and Angelina Jolie lining up to apologize and claim that they just wished they were/fucked two-bit losers like the impotents.

YOUR MOM, THE SWING VOTER

Your mom wants to vote for a Democrat. Every time you talk about politics with her, she mentions a Democratic politician in favorable terms. "He seems so smart. She's just so classy." You tentatively get her to agree with liberal ideas. She's pro-choice. She thought it was terrible what happened to the people stuck in New Orleans. She doesn't see why gays can't get married. She thinks people who are down on their luck could use some help getting back on their feet. She couldn't have put you through school without federal financial aid. But once you cautiously raise the idea of her actually voting for a Democrat, she freezes and goes into denial mode.

What's going on? Your mom isn't dumb. But she is scared to embrace the identity of a liberal, much less of a Democrat, because then people in her community, and perhaps in her own home, will never stop giving her shit about it. You try to talk her into voting Democratic, and she stops you.

Well, don't let up. Your mom is the swing voter we hear so much about—and everyone wonders who this elusive creature is. "Why don't they know who they're going to vote for until the last minute? Are they shallow? Indecisive? What's their problem?" Well, maybe their problem is that they, like your mom, want to vote for Democrats but feel they have to vote for Republicans, and feel torn between what they want to do and what they think they should do, and end up enveloping themselves in the privacy of the voting booth and giving in to one urge or another, depending on what pressure leans hardest on them that day. It feels assholish to lean on your mom, who feels enough pressure as it is, but for the sake of the nation, you really should do it.

Their version of utopia: Republicans stop being giant assholes and start embracing pro-choice views, gay rights, reasonable economic policies, nonaggressive foreign policy, and a decent safety net. This way, your mom could pull a lever for them without breaking a sweat and would never have to deal with pressure from her husband, her neighbors, or you, her yapping liberal child.

GAY RIGHTS UNWILLING LIBERALS

Say you're an uptight yuppie from a wealthy WASP family who loves Jesus but dislikes paying your taxes, unions, and feminist broads. By all measures, you're a born Republican. If people like you start to become an even smaller minority, they'll start making people like you in labs to keep elections interesting. You're the perfect Republican in all ways—except one: You're gay.

In the past, this might not have been such an issue. You could have joined the log cabin Republicans and deluded yourself that sexual orientation doesn't matter in the grand political scheme of things. But nowadays, Republicans run entire campaigns based on the idea that you are the greatest threat to the nation because you unwind at the end of the day with someone who has a set to match yours. You're no liberal, but this puts you in an untenable situation.

You could take the route that Mary Cheney and Andrew Sullivan do, and try to convince conservatives that you're nothing to be scared of. Look! Gay marriage! Is there anything more conservative than wanting to settle down and raise a family? And if you're Mary Cheney, you're rich enough to get away with it. But we watched Andrew Sullivan flail in public for years as a Bush supporter who thought it was just a misunderstanding that kept Republicans from understanding the rightness of gay marriage, before he finally came around and became a huge supporter of Barack Obama. He may swing again, but the lesson should stand: If you're a gay Republican, understand that they really don't want you.

Their version of utopia: The local country club starts advertising its eagerness to host same-sex weddings.

LIBERTARIAN DUDES

This breed is small in real-world terms but appears to be large, both because its members seem to have more time than anyone to spread their message and because they have more funding than anyone else to achieve that goal. Libertarians pride themselves on being more ideologically consistent than anyone else, and perpetually out of power, but the truth is that they are most consistent in voting for Republicans, no matter how strongly Republicans come out against basic civil liberties that year. To gloss over the difference between their self-perception of strong consistency and the outside world's judgment that they're just conservatives who like to smoke pot and get laid, libertarians cope by assuming they're just smarter than everyone else and that's why people don't get them. Ayn Rand appeals to them mostly because they like fairy tales about super-smart people who are oppressed by society through the power of snickering.

Libertarians like to feel besieged on all sides, from the camera-in-your-cooter social conservatives who run the Republican party to the yes-we'll-tax-you-and-we-won't-pretend-otherwise Democratic party. Considering that both parties do end up levying taxes, and that no matter how anti-tax the Republican party claims to be, this never changes (except for with multimillionaires), one would think that libertarians who claim to be splitting the difference would at least go for the party that will protect one set of their issues: personal freedoms. But libertarians rarely convert to Democrats—and, even if it happens, do so grudgingly—which inclines observers to assume that they are just Republicans who resort to the "lesser of two evils" excuse so they can feel sexier and more liberated than their stodgier comrades.

The cornerstone of libertarian ideology is that the government is no good and should just go away. But libertarians are not anarchists, because they'll admit that the government has a few useful functions, invariably ones that make sure hordes of poor and/or brown people don't grab libertarians' shit. They accept that there should be a military and a court system (so that people can sue each other), and police (so that people who want to rob them go to jail). But if the government starts making efforts to rectify injustice in society, suddenly taxes are the worst injustice ever levied against humankind, and denouncing the IRS takes precedence over denouncing segregation, violence against women, or any other piddling, non-tax-related issue.

As much as they claim to be fans of liberty, libertarian dudes will often find state intervention perfectly acceptable when it comes to women's uteruses. By no means are all libertarian dudes anti-choice, but a shockingly high percentage allow that state control over uterine activity is up there with the military, police, and civil courts as legitimate government functions. It's easy to speculate that the reason for this discrepancy might have a lot to do with the crossover between libertarian dudes and level-ten Dungeons & Dragons geekery. We're talking about a lot of guys who suspect they need a shotgun marriage to get any at all, and so don't want the law letting women escape from their drunken mistakes that easily.

Their version of utopia: They're ensconced in their castle, protected from the impoverished masses by a moat and mostly by a giant arsenal of unregulated assault weapons. Throngs of grateful women live in the castle for protection and pay for said protection with sexual favors and chores. There is no need for schools or any other social infrastructure, because the grateful women have to take care of all the shit work to earn their keep. There's no need for a fire department when you live in a castle made of stone.

LADY LIBERTARIANS

Female libertarians mostly resemble the male libertarians, in that they think they're wittier than they are, they feel put upon by a world that doesn't understand their brilliance, and they hate paying their taxes as much as they hate thinking about how society might be too complex for their simplistic answers. But they differ from male libertarians in that pretty much all of them are pro-choice, and they tend to cop to being feminists, because they're just smart enough to realize that saying you're not a feminist is tantamount to saying that you're dumber than men, and libertarians don't think they're dumber than anyone. And when it comes to being unapologetically sexual, libertarian women don't look any different from liberal feminists, though they often fetishize shoes and makeup without feeling guilty about it.

But these are just surface similarities. It's pretty much impossible to find a female libertarian who takes her right to choose (a basic liberty) as seriously as she does her desire to end taxes (a childish fantasy). Abortion-rights issues make voting Republican seem very stupid indeed, and so female libertarians will often resort to "weak people don't deserve my support" arguments, claiming that they don't really need the right to choose because, *unlike some people,* they know how to use birth control. Quarreling with them on this point is equivalent to arguing the inarguable: that these women are ordinary members of human society, which can make mistakes that will be dismissed.

Invocations of the sisterhood of feminists are used strictly for the purpose of self-pity. When called out for supporting politicians who openly oppose women's rights, female libertarians will claim to be victims of discrimination, kicked out of the feminist "club" for daring to be brave, intellectual anti-tax warriors. Take, for example, Megan McArdle, writing for the *Atlantic* in response to some feminist bloggers who had the nerve to make fun of her: "Personally, I'd like to see feminism take on as expansionist a definition as possible without rendering the concept meaningless—something closer to my list than whatever, exactly in the head of people who label me an 'antifeminist.'"

Their version of utopia: Not much different than the guys' version, except they have a seat at the guys' table while the other women wait on them. It's a good life of shooting off guns, being rich, and being told by the men around them that they're so much better than those other women, who don't know how to pull themselves up by their bootstraps. Smarter. Sexier. Better aim. A sterner voice when addressing the help.

"!"

YOU DON'T
HAVE TO BE A
Stinky Hippie to Be an
Environmentalist

CHAPTER ONE

THE DIRTY LITTLE SECRET
of Living Green:
It's Fun

Early in the twenty-first century, it became apparent that status-conscious yuppies had embraced going green as the hot new status symbol. In many ways, it resembles the aerobics craze of the '80s and the yoga craze of the '90s. It only seems simple—in fact, it takes free time, knowledge, and money to do it correctly. You can dish about it at cocktail parties. Most important, it imparts a glow of moral superiority to the enthusiast. Just as a thin waistline speaks of hours working out and denying yourself treats, the hybrid car, the elaborate recycling bin, and the refrigerator full of organic foods purchased at the supermarket speak of deliberate deprivation for the greater good. The rest of Americans indulge every dirty little desire, no matter how environmentally damaging, but the green person thinks only of the future.

Don't believe the hype. The dirty little secret is that many of the recommendations for greening your life are more fun than you'd think. I first clued into how our nation is being suckered into wasteful behavior under the guise of ease or pleasure when I found out about the fancy, green way to heat water: the tankless water heater. These things heat water in the pipes themselves, which is more energy-efficient than the old strategy of holding water in a tank that sucks up energy. If you can afford to install one of these things in your house, you get more than an opportunity to pat yourself on the back: You can also take an excessively long shower without ever running out of hot water, because no tank means no bottom to reach.

When I first learned about this, I was living in a five-hundred-square-foot apartment that had a water heater *under the kitchen counter*. That's right. It was two and a half feet tall. To take a complete shower that involved shaving my pits and lady garden, shampooing and conditioning my hair, soaping and rinsing my body, and washing my face, I had to work in shifts: wash my hair, put in the conditioner, shut off the water. Wait for the heater to fill back up, rinse out my hair while shaving quickly, shut off the water. Wait for the heater to fill back up, then wash my body and face. To fill the bathtub, I'd boil two pots of water and run the bathwater in two shifts. From my perspective, a water heater that never ran out sounded like Paul McCartney's issuing a full apology for his solo career to me personally. With flowers. And a home-cooked vegetarian meal.

That's when I realized that green living, far from being a dreadful sacrifice, was probably all hot showers and Paul McCartney apologies. I couldn't install a tankless water heater, but I could purchase a bicycle and start walking to work instead of driving. After the initial adjustment period, during which I built up the muscle to push over hills on my bicycle without going so slow I felt like I had accidentally reversed time, I discovered that getting out of the car solved a significant percentage of my problems. Who knew that insomnia, cracked teeth, and general irritability can all be traced back to the stress of sitting in traffic behind some asshole who seems to think it's a sport to see if he can get through the green light at the last possible moment so that no one else can make it? On the bicycle or on foot, I could be the first in line to cross with the green light, every single time. It's an impatient egoist's dream.

Also, I don't have to go to the gym anymore. Which means more time for sitting on my ass and writing rants about how awesome bicycles are. Plus, bicycle commuters get to feel mildly superior to everyone. The irritable people envying you inside their cars are but one perk. You can also smile indulgently at the overblown cycling enthusiasts who share the bike lanes with you—the people who probably drove home from work, changed into spandex and super-expensive shoes, and are sitting in front of you at the light, asses in the air and looks of concentration on their faces, in comparison with you, in your jeans, messenger bag, and headphones. Bicycle commuting is like traveling through the world in a bubble of chilled-out–ness.

Environmentally friendly lifestyle choices made life more pleasant for me, barring the weird looks I got from friends and relatives. Leaving the thermostat at eighty degrees in the summer meant learning that I didn't actually have to keep a blanket and sweater on hand just because I'm wearing a T-shirt and shorts. Going to the farmers' market on Saturday mornings and buying random foodstuffs meant that I learned to cook, for one thing, but also, and more important, meant that I knew where to get the orgasmically delicious young cheeses that no one else could find and could take them to parties and gloat. Setting up a recycling bin doubled the amount of space I had to toss garbage away in, meaning I didn't have to take time out of my day for trash runs as often and had more time to download music online and argue with people on blogs. Composting reduced my trash runs even more. Bringing a cloth bag to the grocery store meant I put an end to those painful red marks you get on your hand from the plastic bags. My energy-efficient lightbulbs cost more money up front, but once they were installed, I never had to change a lightbulb again, which was good for me, because sometimes

I'll wait until I've resorted to lighting candles to work up the enthusiasm to haul out a stepladder and confront dried bug corpses to do that task.

One of the best things you can do to go green is to get over the idea that more square footage is better. The less square footage in your house, the less energy you use for heating and air-conditioning, the less lighting you need, and the less you need to vacuum. Which, to my mind, is the real selling point of a small home—less housework. Plus, if you downsize in footage but keep your rent or mortgage budget the same, you can usually get a cooler place, or a place closer to a city, which makes you automatically cooler by osmosis. Plus, you can replace sofas with a bunch of cool vintage chairs and ottomans. Visitors end up sitting on the floor, especially to eat, but this gives your place a bohemian air, especially if you put a candle in a wine bottle for light. (Which is part of the reduce/reuse/recycle mantra, no less.)

For a yuppie affectation, going green turned out to be remarkably cheap, the cheapest trend since calorie reduction in the days before restaurants realized they could charge you more to give you less food. Cutting out the vast majority of driving that happens within a few miles of home means you pay a lot less in gas money—or, if you're really lucky, you can get rid of your car altogether, meaning no insurance or car payments. (Many cities have car-sharing programs, which give you access to a car on the few occasions you need it, for an hourly rate. It's far cheaper than keeping a car if you don't drive much.) Reducing your energy usage lowers your bills, of course. Even using organic food, you'll save money if you stay at home and cook more than you go out to eat. Freeing up more of your income means that you can spend more money on organic beer and wine, or, if you're one of those crazy liberals who take responsibility for themselves as well as for the world, you could probably save it for retirement. If not, you can now afford to get a bunch of new tattoos—and the tattoo removal, too.

THE OTHER DIRTY LITTLE SECRET
of Living Green:
It's Not Enough

As much as I enjoy seeking ways to green up my own life, encourage others to do the same, and reap the benefits of the self-righteous glow it gives me, I also feel kind of guilty (as good liberals should) about doing this. After all, the individual actions of a righteous few can't even balance out the ridiculous, wasteful behavior of most of our uncaring fellow Americans. My vegetarianism doesn't compensate for much when most Americans scarf down more meat than the human body seems able to digest. Riding a bicycle does only so much when the roads are clogged with SUVs whose fuel efficiency is one-half or one-quarter of much smaller cars'. Planting one garden can, at best, counter one suburban McMansion so large that no yard (and therefore no green) can survive. In the grand scheme of things, your little effort is pretty insignificant, so why bother?

When people ask me this, I point out that the direct environmental effect of behavior changes might be minimal, but the social impact can be profound. By riding your bike and taking the bus, you show that it can be done. Planting gardens, recycling, reducing, reusing, vegetarianism—these behaviors impact people around you and help change standards. People need to believe that it can be done, because the next step in cleaning up the environment is pushing through policy, and that will require fighting against the national scourge of whining.

Democracy is the only fair form of government, and it's better than other kinds available, functionally speaking, but it also has the built-in whining issue that makes certain kinds of change practically impossible until major disaster forces people to suck it up. Whining affects both the left and the right, though the right has turned it into an art form—indeed, many whiny conservatives turn their whining into a point of pride. Liberals generally have an air of guilt about them when they insist that they really can't walk half a mile instead of driving, or that they had no choice but to buy a four-bedroom house with vaulted ceilings. Conservatives flaunt their SUVs and buy McMansions as a deliberate "fuck you" to liberals, a form of faux rebellion against people who don't have any real power over them. Both root their rejection of change in the same fear of change, though. Do we really need huge houses, or could we learn to live without coffee tables and overstuffed sofas? We won't know until we try, or until we see someone else pull it off without being worse off for it.

Change is hard, and most people don't undertake it willingly. Grasping this fundamental fact is the first step on the road to being a liberal who looks at policy as a way to shape people's behavior. Ironically, you'd think that conservatives would grasp the resistance to change that most people exhibit, because they exhibit the most fear about change. But it's liberals who point out that if we wait until half the population stops driving and starts bicycling without trying to persuade them with a mix of carrots and sticks, then we might as well start investing in water-purifying machines and sunscreen, because there will be no stopping a global warming–related Armageddon.

The summer of 2008 showed how well people can respond to a poke in the ass from a stick, a stick in the form of $4-a-gallon gasoline. In fact, to make it clear how complicit I am, I didn't even bother selling my truck until gas got that expensive. Oh, I used my bike more than my truck at that point, so I wasn't completely lazy, but that meant that I filled up my tank maybe once every two months. So when I had to do it and face that $50 bill at the gas station, I decided then and there to sell my truck and force myself to find cheaper ways to get around. (Helps that I have my boyfriend's car to borrow when I want to buy a bunch of twelve-packs of soda.) The kick in the ass worked on me, and on others. Even though we'd been told that people drive only because they have no other choice, rising gas prices produced a dramatic drop in the number of miles people put in behind the wheel each month.

But compared with what needs to happen to save the environment—and ourselves from a zombie movie–like future—even quadrupling gas prices won't do the trick. The entire system's been built on wastefulness that we can't afford anymore, and anything short of rethinking the entire system and making massive changes will do nothing more than stave off the tragic consequences for a few more years. For many elderly Republicans in Congress who plan to die soon enough, that may not mean much to them, but for the rest of us, this should matter.

Up until recently, most people seemed to have a sense that massive, complex systems couldn't collapse, because their very size held them up. The energy-wasting, space-sucking suburban sprawl and all its interconnecting highways seem as inevitable to us as trees, sky, and people who meander down the sidewalk without moving to the side so you can pass them, and it doesn't even seem possible that the whole system could fall apart simply because of something like sustained high gas prices. But Americans got a big wake-up call with the economic collapse, which showed how easily a big system like, say, our entire banking industry could crumble because of one bad investment scheme (subprime-mortgage lending combined with credit default swaps). This is a rare opportunity. People believe disaster can strike, so they're open to hearing about huge changes to prevent it.

So, instead of environmentalists' pushing small, incremental changes that will take forever to implement and might not do enough to reduce pollution, resource depletion, and global warming, maybe it's time to push for big change. What if we could cut suburban sprawl by 50 percent? Make cars optional for most people, and other, cleaner forms of transportation preferable for most? What if we could really move toward using alternative-energy sources before the world's oil runs out? If there was ever a time to strike, it's during these next few years of upheaval.

ATKINS:
An Environmental Disaster

Few things point to the way Americans dichotomize and turn on each other with ease than the concurrent trends of vegetarianism and the Atkins diet. They certainly have made many a family outing awkward—at least, if you're in my family and trying to find a restaurant that will serve both the people who eschew meat eating and the people who eschew eating anything that isn't meat. (Most Southern-cooking places will do—the Atkins fans can load up on barbecue while the veggies make do with a baked potato and some cornbread.) These divergent leanings mirror the concurrent, divided enthusiasm over Hummers and hybrid cars. The two groups attracted to the two different trends probably think they don't have much in common, but they share the American faith in consumption choices to identify themselves, make a profound statement, and even change the world.

Fun as it is to mock people who self-righteously drive a Prius to Whole Foods to buy a bucket of hummus, Hummer drivers are undeniably the bigger assholes, because what they're advertising is that they aggressively don't care and will gladly shit on the planet to prove that they can. You have this author's full permission to make endless fun of people who bought Hummers that get three miles to the gallon, only to see gas prices rise and discover that no one would buy their unwieldy, piece-of-shit cars.

Unlike the Hummer, the Atkins diet doesn't have a "be an asshole—it's fun" selling point. No, its tagline is more subtle: "Be an asshole—it's surprisingly good for your waistline." The Atkins has the same hook as articles in your newspaper's science section about how eating a box of chocolates that you down with a bottle of wine will prevent cancer—which is to say, it adds some scientific-sounding stuff to wishful thinking and sells it to you in the form of a $14.95 trade paperback. Prior to the Atkins trend, Americans already ate a bunch of meat, and it had that asshole allure to it, where you were both enjoying the flavor of meat and sticking it to the hippies. But, as always happens when you stick it to the hippies, you guiltily believed you would pay eventually for your immoral pseudorebellion. You also believed (correctly) that sucking down piles of greasy meat tends to lead to thickening waistlines. So of course you were happy to hear that it wasn't the meat at all, but the innocuous bun that it came in—a bun that was made with zero abuse or murder of animals, making it perilously close to hippie food—that was making you fat.

From what I've read, it's not crazy to think that skipping carbs will help you lose weight. Knocking off a portion of the food on your plate always lowers the amount of calories you consume, and it doesn't really matter which calories you choose. In other words, a hamburger without its bun obviously has fewer calories than a hamburger with its bun. You don't need to believe in the evil mojo of carbs to see the logic of this.

But if you have to push a fad diet that's about eliminating an entire food group and all its calories, why do you have to eliminate the one that both costs the least and doesn't do near as much damage to the environment as meat does? Environmentally speaking, we already eat way too much meat, and the last thing we needed as a country was a trend toward eating even *more* of it.

Ask any environmentalist about the problem with meat eating, and we can drone for hours about it. Meat requires substantially more land to develop than grain does, because first you have to grow the grain, and then you have to feed it to the animals before you eat them. It's an incredibly inefficient system that's the caloric equivalent of taking four right turns instead of one left turn. And every stage you add to the process of getting energy from the ground into your mouth means hauling a bunch of stuff around in trucks, spewing pollution into the air. Producing meat actually adds more carbon to the atmosphere than cars do. Agricultural subsidies' support of cheap meat means that farmers are encouraged to grow nothing but corn, since they can get it subsidized as animal feed, but it also means that Americans have shockingly little diversity in our diets, since most of what we eat was originally corn.

Even cow farts are a problem. Farts add methane gas to the atmosphere, which adds to the global-warming problem. Before you cast disdain on a veggie burger, remember that it never once farted on its way to your plate. And if you're worried about the people farts you'll emit if you eat it, you always have Beano and Gas-X. But if it still keeps you up at night, remember this: Even if you subsist entirely on a diet of broccoli and beans, there's no way in hell you could ever fart as much as a cow, even if you have a remarkably large colon.

The fact that so many Americans signed up for the Atkins diet without even stopping for a moment to consider that eating almost nothing but meat might be just the kind of wastefulness that's put the human race on a collision course to environmental disaster is the sort of thing that makes liberals suggest weakly that we may have an education gap about these political issues. Attempts to bridge it might hit the echo-chamber wall. Sure, we have books like Michael Pollan's *The Omnivore's Dilemma* and Mark Bittman of *The New York Times* talking endlessly about the downsides of meat consumption, and the liberal-foodie community's attempts to find creative ways to significantly reduce meat consumption while still eating well. But these efforts are unlikely to reach beyond the circles of people who were already hostile to the notion of dieting by piling two pounds of meat on their plates but skipping the bread.

Unfortunately, efforts to bridge the gap between vegetarianism, or at least meat reducing, and the general public have been dominated by the worst possible people, a.k.a. animal-rights nuts who seem to be fond of mild anorexia. The *Skinny Bitch* book series had a similar splash with the public that the Atkins had before it, and you could practically hear the authors giggling to each other in self-congratulation over how they tricked so many women into being vegans *without even knowing it.* Because that was the point of the books—just in case their implicitly scolding women into being ashamed for having an ounce of flesh on their bodies wasn't offensive enough, the authors also think you're stupid and won't clue in pretty quickly to the fact that they're the sort of vegans who skip even honey because they feel sorry for the poor bees. (This, by the way, is a really bad attitude to have if you care about the environment at all—bees are necessary to pollinate crops, but populations of wild bees are dwindling. If it weren't for beekeepers who make a living selling honey, we might be facing some level of crisis on the agricultural front, and your home garden wouldn't be doing so well, either.)

Selling eating disorder–level thinking coupled with environmentally deaf wackadoodle veganism while trying to trick people seems like a poor trade-off for pushing overconsumption of meat as a magic diet. It does make you wonder if Americans are congenitally incapable of choosing the moderate path of restraining themselves without falling headlong into self-deprivation, by embracing either vegetarianism or at least severely reduced meat consumption but not doing weird stuff like turning the eating of honey into a test of morality.

If there's any way to get us on that path, it has to be by selling moderate self-restraint as an environmental choice, instead of as the magic bullet to get women into that sexy bathing suit by Memorial Day. We're not so thoroughly self-centered that we can't make changes for the greater good. We recycle and use energy-saving lightbulbs and appliances. We buy organic, and even the proud assholes among us have started to reconsider their love of gas-guzzling SUVs. We even take public subways and light rail if they're available. So perhaps direct appeals about planetary health, instead of guilt-laden attempts to deceive, could work.

GROW YOUR OWN WAY:
Gardening for Food, Gardening against Global Warming

All the hip kids are going green. Once a sweet-looking hybrid car hit the market and Al Gore remade himself from the old fuddy-duddy whose wife wanted to sticker naughty music into the global climate's Hollywood-beloved protector, you could start counting down the minutes until environmental friendliness became as mandatory as liking Nirvana was in the '90s (and in both cases, damn straight). Environmentalism used to connote dirty-hippie self-deprivation practices, like flushing the toilet only after taking a shit but demurring if you merely urinated. But now it has fresh, shiny, modern, hip implications.

Organic gardening has benefited from this hipster makeover. Just a few years ago, the phrase "organic gardening" brought to mind tiny, bug-eaten vegetables served over tasteless brown rice for dinner, paired with herbal tea instead of a decent glass of wine. But now you can proudly put an organic wine on the table to go with the fancy dinner you made from a hip new cookbook recipe, using nothing but organic vegetables from the farmers' market, and everyone will rave about how much more flavor you get from organic produce. Even *The New York Times* has a vegan-friendly, organic-pimping food blogger. In less than a decade, organic gardening has gone from being a misunderstood hippie pastime to being the only way to go. Now, people who once thought growing houseplants was too much responsibility are looking to build organic gardens, even if the only space they have for one is in a corner of their fire escape. Among my friends who have gotten into gardening (and its inevitable partner hobby, foodie-ism, which is like cooking on steroids), you will never hear the evil words "Miracle-Gro" pass through their lips. On the other hand, "fish emulsion" has become a topic for polite conversation.

In other words, organic gardening has moved away from being the sole property of patchouli-drenched hippies and church ladies who compete to see who can grow the fussiest version of the rose of the moment, as crowned by *Southern Living* magazine.

If you haven't jumped on this bandwagon, I highly recommend you consider it. Naturally, not everyone has the time, physical ability, or space to garden, but if you have thought about working around some of your current obstacles, now's the time to pounce. A few years ago, intrepid would-be urban gardeners had to figure out everything on their own, but now, thanks to green trends and the Internet, you have a ton of help. Googling "urban gardening" turns up forty-four million hits. Looking for ways to squeeze green into the urban landscape has become the cool thing for both individuals and city planners to do, and it's resulted in innovations like green roofing, where the tops of buildings are turned into landscaping or even gardening spaces. The art of container gardening has exploded, and now once-unusual strategies, like growing tomatoes upside down or setting up a permanent herb garden in your kitchen, have become commonplace.

Gardening has gotten so hip that some people who've mastered the beginning levels have started to add elements to their garden, like beehives or chickens. This is recommended only if you have protective gear, a real yard (chickens and bees do not like fire escapes), and patient neighbors.

Learning to garden has many short- and long-term advantages. In the short term, you get tons of fresh basil and maybe even some fresh tomatoes. In the long term, you learn valuable farming skills that will help after the zombie apocalypse wipes out most of humanity and you and Brad Pitt have to start rebuilding the human race in the one corner of the planet that managed to survive relatively unscathed. Your gardening skills at this point will turn what could have been a tragic event into a real chance for humanity to get a fresh start, especially now that global warming has been halted and reversed, since its main source stopped polluting when their brains disappeared into the guts of zombies. Sure, you and Brad will miss both the tabloid press and Angelina, but in your hearts, you'll know it was for the best—as long as you have something to eat now, which you will, because you practiced growing tomatoes on your balcony.

In the unlikely event that a zombie apocalypse doesn't wipe out all of humanity, then global warming will remain a pressing problem. Luckily, you and your humble but growing plant population will help out in this potential future as well. How? Well, if you're really serious about being a good liberal, you should have already paid money to let Al Gore scare you about global warming in his documentary *An Inconvenient Truth,* but if you haven't yet, I'll let you off the hook if you put down this book, go rent it, and then come back to finish this chapter.

Back, slacker? Wasn't that movie a lot more entertaining than you thought a documentary based on a PowerPoint presentation could be? Being a good liberal who cares about saving the world is not the eye-rolling bore that Rush Limbaugh leads people to believe. In fact, since it's the first line of defense against turning into George Will, that alone should recommend it in terms of bore protection.

But I digress. And after I take one more potshot at George Will—can you believe that fuck monkey thinks man-made global warming is a myth?—I'll continue.

If you were paying attention, you heard the part where Al Gore said that you can help by planting plants, which convert carbon dioxide to oxygen. It's true that you personally won't be able to reverse global warming by planting one tree, but collectively, it sure can help. Believe me, if you followed my instructions to watch this movie, you'll probably be doing what I did right afterward: completely covering every inch of sun-accessible space you can with greenery in the hope that you can somehow stave off impending disaster. And then you'll stand in the middle of your urban jungle, breathing in the heavily oxygenated air, feeling for a moment like you've created your own atmosphere-cleaning mini-factory, until you realize that breathing in deeply means you're actually reversing the effects by sucking in oxygen and blowing out carbon dioxide.

At this point, you should calm down and think about this: Gardening does more for the environment than an immediate and minor carbon dioxide–cleanup campaign does. Growing fruits and vegetables does more than prepare you for the zombie apocalypse. Every fruit or vegetable that you buy at the grocery store, though it does contribute to your personal bottom-line health, takes its toll on the planet. It took fossil fuel–burning methods to fertilize it, and it burned fossil fuels to get to the store, often from faraway places like South America.

All that fossil fuel burning is cut out if you grow your produce at home using organic fertilizers, and the journey from plant to plate requires only your own two legs. Organic fertilizer helps the environment, too, because it's recycled from stuff that would otherwise be thrown into a landfill. This is true whether you do your own composting or buy compost from an organic manufacturer, which you may have to do if you don't have space to compost. If you plant in the ground, you help reduce soil erosion. More to the point, urban gardening normalizes the idea that green should be sprouting from every place possible in an urban landscape and will help clean up the air and make life just a tad more pleasant.

Outside of the political reasons to get into organic gardening, I have to admit that it has more personal benefits than even the most pleasurable of other green trends. Even people who were fussy kids who didn't like touching dirt will find that as grown-ups, they enjoy digging their hands into it. What's awesome about plants is that they're the cleanest dirty thing you'll find. Dirt will get under your fingernails, but it feels like good, clean dirt. Going outside to dig around and weed and then coming in to take a nice, hot shower and turn yourself from Farmer Jane into Sexy Miss Urbanite in a Miniskirt is a pleasure that's hard to equal with any other simple activity. You can dig in the dirt where the grubs hang out, then wash up and sit outside with your growing plant family, breathing in the clean air.

Gardening is also the perfect way to work out that most fucked-up of human desires: the desire to nurture life. Babies are pains in the ass that just grow into bigger pains in the ass, dogs pee on the floor, and cats sit on your head while you're sleeping and stare at you with a look that says, *If you died right now, I could eat you.* Plants help scratch your itch to nurture without making you endure these drawbacks. Even better, you can just keep adding more and more plants to your collection without becoming a crazy cat lady or having to get a reality show on cable television to pay your bills, and you can feel good about it to boot, because, unlike cats or kids, plants give back more than they take.

And then there's composting. My boyfriend makes fun of me for enjoying composting, but it's the dirty little semisecret of organic garden-ers: Getting a really good compost pile going is a near erotic pleasure in its earthy perfection. When you turn it over and see all sorts of earthworms scrambling back into the habitat you've built especially for them, even the most hardened cynic will glow with that dirty-hippie pleasure of being one with the planet and all that crap. You'll start saying things like, "When I die, I don't want to be cremated or buried in a coffin. I want to go back to the earth, so I can come back as some flowers or even some zucchini," and people will look at you funny, and you won't care, because you'll be that in tune with the rhythms of the planet, at least some of the time.

This in turn will help make you a better environmentalist, because once you start digging your hands in the dirt and really getting to know it, you'll begin to feel a little bit more attached to the planet, and that will make you want to save it all that much more.

"REDUCE,
REUSE, RECYCLE"
Reaches Its Sexiness Peak

Hopefully, if you've read everything up to this point, you don't need much convincing that going green is the hot new thing to do. And while a good liberal like me must consider the recent economic collapse to be nothing but a complete tragedy that will end up eating up the working class even as the rich get most of the press because they have to spend less on diamonds, at least the recession means that the new frugality trend dovetails nicely with the environmentalism trend.

For decades now, the environmentalist motto has been "Reduce, Reuse, Recycle." At first, employing this philosophy in your daily life is hard, but if you practice, it becomes second nature. You start off reducing by bringing your own bag to the grocery store, and next thing you know, you're becoming a pro at finding ways to buy life's necessities with a whole lot less packaging. Reusing starts off with your turning the grocery bags you do get into trash-can liners, and before you know it, you're turning coffee cans into planters and whipping out the sewing machine to remake all the clothes you're tired of into brand-new, cool outfits. Recycling brings to mind images of a pile of smushed-up cans in a blue trash bin, but once you get into the habit, you start to incorporate funky variations, like buying vintage clothing.

The biggest downside to trendy environmentalism (outside of the fear that it may die, as trends often do) is that it can make you think you need to spend a buttload of cash. But if you're spending a ton of money on your environmentalism, you're doing it wrong. It should be *saving* you money. In fact, more than any other factor, that potential for saving money is what has driven people I know to adopt environmentalist habits. Biking instead of driving saves on gas. Buying an album for $2 on vinyl instead of paying $18 for the same thing on a new CD saves you money and reduces waste. Turning the air-conditioning down and supplementing with fans saves on electrical bills. Walking and biking everywhere often means you can let that gym membership lapse. Garage sales instead of the mall, cheap plastic rewashable cups instead of paper ones, finding creative ways to reuse stuff you'd throw away instead of buying new stuff to fill that need—hard as it may be to believe, the hippest lifestyle trend in America right now is one that actually saves you money. There's no excuse not to capitalize on it.

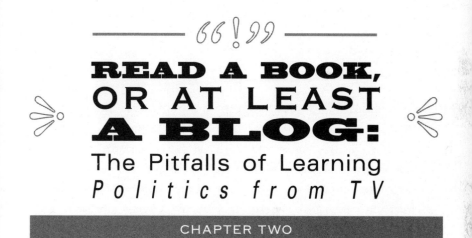

READ A BOOK, OR AT LEAST A BLOG:
The Pitfalls of Learning
Politics from TV

CHAPTER TWO

"FAIR AND BALANCED," My Ass

When picking a mini-chapter title that involves the phrase "fair and balanced" with the intention of mocking the phrase "fair and balanced," a writer goes to war with herself. On the one hand, the choice isn't very original. In fact, mocking the phrase "fair and balanced" now counts for over 50 percent of the uses of the phrase "fair and balanced." On the other hand, you want to grab on to that phrase because of its evocative nature, so evocative that it seems almost designed for ironic reclaiming.

"Fair and balanced," of course, originated with Fox News, the only major cable news station that doesn't try to be either of these two things but functions mainly as a right-wing propaganda channel. That everyone knows this doesn't mean they come out and admit it. The first rule of right-wing propagandizing is, you don't talk about right-wing propagandizing. You obscure your true mission under a thick blanket of ideological dog whistles and outright lies. "States' rights" means "a return to legal segregation." Being "pro-life" has nothing to do with improving life; it means that someone would like to throw women in jail for a choice one-third of them make. "Fiscal conservatism" means "ruining the economy by sucking the government dry with corporate giveaways." So, of course, "fair and balanced" means "right-wing propaganda."

But conservative audiences who embraced the phrase didn't mind this transparent lie, probably because the phrase had emotional reverberations with them. Like much in the world of the right wing, "fair and balanced" is a code phrase that refers to a larger and well-rehearsed argument. In this case, the argument was that the mainstream media is hopelessly biased toward a liberal point of view.

The critique goes something like this: The mainstream media is biased toward liberalism, and not just because liberals are much less likely to be fantasists who have no respect for reality. No, it's because mainstream-media types have college degrees and drink fancy coffee drinks, which makes them members of the liberal elite and unable to relate to you, the average Joe, who presumably waited until your wedding and believes in demonic possession. They're also biased because they don't run Republican-party press releases as news as often as they should, which should be 100 percent of the time.

This critique, which Eric Alterman labeled the "so-called liberal media theory," creates in thinking people a range of reactions, from coughing politely in their sleeves to guffawing loudly. The corporate-owned media has no discernible motivation in pushing leftist politics, and, more to the point, has a demonstrable habit of currying favor with right-wingers, in that it will allow people to spout scientifically demonstrable nonsense to be "balanced." To those of us who consider anti-racism and feminism integral parts of liberalism, the sea of white male faces on TV alone demonstrates the silliness of complaining that the mainstream media leans liberal.

But the complaint's pseudopopulist implications strike deep at the heart of the worst insecurities of the upper-middle-class professionals who control the mainstream media. They feel the pain of not being "street" or, more to the point, "haystack" enough, and the more phony guilt trips from millionaires like Rush Limbaugh or their own effete members, like David Brooks, they get, the harder they strive to put more right-wing lunatics on the air and treat them like they're not crazy, as if that will relax the criticism instead of just encourage the right-wing media to redouble its efforts until it takes over completely. The result? A media that leans harder and harder to the right all the time. A media environment where Pat Buchanan rarely has to deal with anyone noting that he's a creationist with the kind of racist opinions that make you fear taking your grandparents out in public. A media environment where friends of white supremacists can call Barack Obama a "socialist" on TV without getting called on it or being politely uninvited on the legitimate grounds that no one that stupid should be asked to appear as an "expert."

None of the concessions to ceaseless right-wing complaints about the liberal media have done a thing to stem the tide of those complaints. Instead, these concessions mean that we have a circuslike atmosphere of unreality in the mainstream media, and if the electoral consequences weren't so deadly, it would be funnier—the way *Saturday Night Live* is funny, not like how *Fargo* was funny. The strong conservative bent in the mainstream media really revealed itself during the early days of Barack Obama's administration, over the fight to pass a stimulus bill to save our faltering economy.

In an objective media, instead of a "fair and balanced" media, the package would have been analyzed the same way the congressional budget office analyzed it: How much spending where, and what will it get us? Boring questions, I suppose, but, more important, questions that led to answers that conservatives found ideologically incorrect. Social spending tends to generate more national wealth, for the same reason that spending money on your company's infrastructure tends to improve your business and makes you more money. Health care spending improves productivity because well people miss less work than sick people. That's the sort of common sense that makes conservatives crap their pants, and for good reason. After all, if people start to accept some aspects of reality, such as "people with jobs have more money to spend than those who don't," then you might start accepting other reality-based beliefs, such as evolutionary theory and that condoms stop the transmission of HIV.

Instead of a sober assessment of the cost and benefits of the bill, we got many news cycles of hand-wringing because Barack Obama had "failed" at bipartisanship, because he couldn't get any Republicans to vote for his bill, even though he called many personally and begged. It was never explained why bipartisanship was such a marvelous value, and why only Democrats had a responsibility to carry it out. (Which was the implication, since Republicans were the only ones who stopped any bipartisanship, while all the blame fell on Obama's shoulders.) The narrative in the mainstream media didn't make any sense unless people accepted that the media has to lean hard to the right in an effort to avoid being called pansy-ass liberals by right-wingers it fears in the same way nerds have always feared bullies.

If the result were just that Americans kept foolishly voting against our own self-interest because we don't get a fair representation of the parties, that would be bad enough. But the "fair and balanced" problem does more than that. With all this skittish concern over the dangers facing anyone who speaks the truth on TV, much less expresses a liberal viewpoint to counterbalance all the conservative voices, we have a media that continues to get weirder and dumber. And that steady diet of the news equivalent of junk food is giving the nation a case of mental diabetes.

KNOWING WHO TO VOTE FOR
Shouldn't Require Sixty Hours of Research

When traveling the highways and byways of liberalism, one often comes across curmudgeonly television haters who bemoan the fact that other Americans don't spend nearly as much time as they do boning up on the literary minutia of the current political landscape. It's a maddening stance and a lazy scold, because these people just know that they won't meet with much resistance. Few people are going to stand up for reading less and getting all one's information from TV. It's like trying to find someone who'll defend a diet consisting solely of Doritos.

You won't find a defender of the book- and newspaper-free intellectual diet here, of course. Ideally, most people would take their intellectual life and citizenship responsibilities seriously enough to immerse themselves in enough information that they could, in a pinch, take on a job as a congressional representative without panicking. (Of course, many of our fine congressmen, especially from the South, appear to have no problem taking on that job without knowing enough to read the instructions on a toaster oven, so perhaps this isn't setting the bar high enough.) But the fact that this doesn't happen doesn't point to a severe lack of fortitude in the American character, or a malevolent hatred of taking on citizenship responsibilities, especially since many of these ill-informed people do take the time to go out and vote.

Instead of assuming laziness, I'd argue that many Americans would like to be better informed, but they don't have the time to sit down and read enough to really understand the issues in-depth. The average American schmo gets up at 6:00 AM (or earlier), gets out of the house by 7:00 AM, sits for an hour in traffic (or more) to get to work, works until 5:00 PM (or later), sits in traffic for an hour, and gets home at 6:00 PM (or later). Then they have chores to do, children to parent, and dinner to make, and maybe even want to work in a little time for exercise so their sedentary life doesn't kill them. After all that, if they want to sit down and veg out in front of the TV, who can blame them?

Even with all this pressure on them, many Americans do try to remember their citizenship duties and flip the channel to the nightly news or a cable news network in an attempt to multitask by turning vegging-out time into political-education time. If this weren't so, these shows wouldn't get the ratings to justify their existence, and entire networks dedicated to politics would die without breathing in their life-giving advertising oxygen.

But instead of seeing the American enthusiasm for news shows as evidence that they do care enough to make an effort with the energy they've got left from working and living, we prefer to scold them and tell them they should do more. By indulging this criticism, though, you automatically turn yourself into a hypocrite. You're scolding others for laziness, but you yourself are too lazy to find a better way to feel self-righteous than by jumping all over people for behaviors you know damn well will never change—well, unless we move toward a thirty-five-hour workweek or create an efficient commuter system that gets people home mere minutes after they leave work, so traffic doesn't drain them of all will to live.

The "people watch too much TV" judgment assumes that it's easier to guilt-trip nearly three hundred million people into changing their habits, many of which are ingrained out of economic necessity, than it is to ask news shows to do a better job of educating people, particularly about policy debates and candidate stances. This seems a rather irrational assumption from a group of anti-TV people who think of themselves as highly rational critical thinkers. From a sheer numbers standpoint, there are exponentially fewer people to convince in news TV production than in the entire country, and, of course, it's much easier to get a hold of major media outlets than it is to reach every single overworked Joe Blow in the country.

We can flatter ourselves and say, "But surely candidate positions and policy debates are way too complex to be reduced to television sound bites." This might be true, but we don't actually know this for sure, because it appears that most TV news shows don't even try to explain the issues in straightforward terms. Mostly, they seem to avoid straightforward reporting altogether, instead preferring to run stories on the dangers of young people having genitals, the behavior of out-of-control celebrities, and crimes that have no larger meaning. When they do meander over to politics, they tend to cover D.C. politics like it's an episode of *Gossip Girl*—who got this advantage over whom, who made this faux pas that the opposing party can pretend to find offensive, whose wife wore what.

What little time is left to actually address issues and candidate positions consists of partisans from either side of an issue (or, more commonly, a centrist and a conservative) "debating" the issue or the candidate for two minutes by shouting over each other, with little to no intervention from the hosts if someone just starts lying or refusing to let the other person speak. Thus, ill-informed people tune in to squeeze some information into their busy days, and they're as likely as not to hear some right-wing lies that they believe are true, because there's no one stepping in to correct the record. If we hear much from the candidates at all, it's in quick sound bites that are usually selected for their inanity.

As much as I'd like every American to be able to jump up and serve as a politician in a pinch, the truth is that most of us don't need to know more than who to vote for. Such a decision shouldn't require sixty hours of watching a bunch of partisans shout at each other between segments on the newest teenage sex crazes and what Lindsay Lohan is doing with her pussy this week. Nor should it really require extensive reading. All it really requires is an efficient, facts-based breakdown of candidate positions that could be sufficiently absorbed over a couple of months of the campaign, broken down into short (but fact-heavy) segments on the nightly news. If people had access to that kind of knowledge, they'd probably go into the voting booth better informed than someone who watches endless hours of cable news networks as they stand currently.

For people who find this appalling, the precedent actually exists—not in the world of TV, but in the much vaunted newspapers, which have featured endorsements and inserts briefly describing candidate positions and using facts, instead of letting a bunch of people bullshit and expecting the voters to figure out which bullshit they distrust the least. (Newspapers save that for their op-ed page.)

Better TV instead of no TV sounds like a weak-minded compromise, but at this point, we're in an emergency ignorance situation, and something is better than nothing. The right-wing publication *Conservative HQ* found that 91 percent of its readership actually believes that Barack Obama is a socialist, a fascist, or a communist—something the magazine's editors trumpeted, but that outsiders correctly saw as evidence of Americans' resounding ignorance. Ninety-one percent of any group shouldn't believe such obvious bullshit, unless they live in a bubble where their ignorance is never refuted. Cable TV coddles that sort of ignorance, but it doesn't have to.

WHO SAYS A LIBERAL
Can't Get the Ratings?

It's hard to even remember a time before Fox News started to clog up the cable streams and the minds of the already weak-minded. People bitched and moaned about the negative effect TV news had on the average voter, of course, but their complaints seem quaint, even sweet, compared with the problems that Fox News introduced into marketplace. Sure, people worried about how TV news, particularly cable news, chose the visually interesting over the truly important, and how the need to keep it moving meant that the length of time anyone had to impart information or make a point fell well below the sixty-second mark.

Like I said, sweet and really kind of harmless compared with the evil Fox News unleashed. For some reason, it seems it has occurred to no one that a right-wing propaganda outfit disguised as the news could erupt from the depths of Rupert Murdoch's coffers, but unfortunately, it turned out that a solid number of Americans really wanted such a thing. George Orwell miscalculated when he imagined the Two Minute Hate—Fox News showed you could have a 24/7 Hate, and, worse, that people would actually watch Bill O'Reilly. Despite its being loud, annoying, and stupid, Fox

News began to kick ass in the ratings, and other news outlets started to panic. And it's safe to assume that it must be Fox News's right-wing bent that accounted for its success.

Watching O'Reilly alone can give a person that impression. It creates in the viewer a feeling somewhere between that of being lectured by an insufferable older relative and that of being screamed at by a ratty street-corner crank. Even before O'Reilly was sued for sexually harassing an employee by forcing her to engage in phone sex with him, during which he offered to scrub her "boobs" (his word) with a falafel, even the most marginally aware viewer could spot him as a pervert, with his endless tirades about Girls These Days, with their sexy this and abortion that—tirades that seamlessly blended moral outrage with visible titillation.

With this in mind, it's understandable that other cable news channels thought it was such right-wing nuttery that drew the ratings, because it sure as hell couldn't be the charm or the hosts or the programming style. Add to that the election of George W. Bush, and one could make a case that America had basically gone to the wingnut dogs. It was morally reprehensible, yes, but TV is a business, so other cable news networks could skip that consideration and try to compete by being perhaps not *more* right wing than Fox, but at least competitively right wing.

Thus began the dark days of cable network news, when you could find hosts who varied from being mildly right-leaning centrists to being mouth-breathing wingnuts, and your average liberal opinion-maker had a better chance of getting on *The O'Reilly Factor*, only to get her microphone cut, than she did of appearing on networks that were more supposedly mainstream.

The network that is now reputedly the most liberal, MSNBC, introduced a supposedly wide range of hosts, from wingnut Republican Joe Scarborough to Blue Dog Democrat Chris Matthews, whose main claim to fame was shifting from humoring conservative Republicans to actually challenging them a solid 5 percent of the time, when they went from nutty to off-the-charts bizarre. Sadly, MSNBC even took a short detour into giving Michael Savage his own TV show, even though he is such an enormous right-wing bigot that he was actually banned from the U.K. (He lasted a full four months before getting fired for telling a caller to get AIDS and die.)

MSNBC clearly didn't have the stomach for that level of conservative vitriol. It takes an unflinching level of assholishness to cut it in the right-wing media, as Bill O'Reilly has shown repeatedly. For instance, O'Reilly took a shine to demonizing Kansas-based doctor and abortion provider George Tiller. Tiller was also a favorite target of anti-choice nuts, who victimized the good doctor with more than one attempt at murder, one of which ended in serious injury to him. Despite this history, O'Reilly dedicated twenty-nine separate show segments to Dr. Tiller, comparing him to the Nazis, accusing him of lying about medical indicators for abortion, and implying that the doctor killed babies for fun. But when a right-wing nut took O'Reilly's word and murdered Dr. Tiller during church services, O'Reilly unflinchingly took to the airwaves to wave off responsibility and then recant the doctor's "sins" to imply that he had deserved to die.

There's coloring outside the moral lines for profit, and then there's what Fox News does. MSNBC decided to change its tune a little and experiment with giving Keith Olbermann, a former sports journalist, his own show where he could start to do something unheard of on TV—spout off on the news from a liberal point of view. At the time, the common perception was that such a show was doomed to fail. Deep down in their hearts, the much maligned coastal elitists who run the networks believed that the unwashed flyover states hated liberals as much as Rush Limbaugh coached them to, and that no liberal could really pull decent ratings.

That idea didn't die overnight, but it did start to lose its will to live, and it finally received its death blow when Olbermann started beating O'Reilly in the ratings, in June 2008. MSNBC realized that it couldn't beat Fox at its own game, but that it could play competitively by changing its strategies a bit, so it made the incredibly bold move of making Rachel Maddow, a wonkish lesbian with a history that included time on the definitely liberal Air America radio network, the host of her own show and the personal hero of millions.

Maddow also raised the ratings, and those of us who thought cable news was doomed were pleasantly surprised when it enjoyed a brief period of liberal glory in the run-up to the 2008 presidential election. We could turn on CNN or MSNBC and see genuinely intelligent liberals permitted to express themselves without being shouted down! CNN even got into the game by giving Campbell Brown her own show, which was perceived as liberal by virtue of her seeming smart and not full of shit. Suddenly, the news networks seemed to accept that the fact that the parties split most national campaigns almost evenly is a good reason to believe that perhaps the entire nation isn't a sea of undifferentiated wingnuttery, and that they could pull ratings with more liberal content.

Can it last? A quick search of news stories on ratings indicates that the explosion of highly rated liberal news programs in 2008 is showing signs of slowing down, but then again, all political content and programming loses a huge portion of its audience during election down-seasons. And maybe there's a small sliver of truth to the idea that liberals just don't watch as much TV news as conservatives, for reasons that can't really make this liberal feel bad. After all, liberals are younger, hipper, more interested in diversity, and less fearful, all traits that get them out of the house, or at least motivate them to spend their leisure time in myriad ways, instead of sitting on the couch, grousing about political opinions they formed based on a minimal amount of information. There's sex to be had and video games to be played, and reading and actually understanding stuff to be done, which are exactly the sort of "elitist" pastimes that right-wing pundits like to bash. Let's face it—deep down inside, most of us liberals wanted more liberal talk shows not because we intended to be avid viewers, but because we hoped they would lead some fence-sitters away from their meaner and stupider urges and toward the light.

But even if liberal programming can't ever really compete, it still gets ratings, damnit, and more ratings than networks like MSNBC would get trying to compete in the wingnut game with shameless pros, like Fox News has. Perhaps the music and publishing industries could be a model for liberal television's success: Intelligent, independent books and records will never sell like the latest Dan Brown novel or Britney Spears dreck, but they can do all right by trying to attract a different audience.

DON'T TURN
THE TV OFF—
Turn Yourself On

TV, which appeals to short attention spans and lack of in-depth understanding of issues, isn't going anywhere. And admit it: You don't really care. Oh, you may say you do, as you clink your cocktail glass full of expensive scotch while adamantly insisting on your love of a more intelligent political atmosphere to your friends. But when you come home from work and plop down on the couch with a glass of apple juice and cheap brandy, you have to confess that you just want to turn on *The Daily Show* and feel like you're at least a little more caught up than you would be otherwise.

Aw, hell, the anti-TV mentality has lost a lot of its allure, so admitting this in public, with or without scotch, is the new, hip version of saying you don't even have a TV. And admitting you love Jon Stewart is the new version of saying you listen only to NPR, and not to those hee-hawing morning comedy shows. But deep down inside, we all wish people read and thought about subjects in a little more depth. I want badly to say that reading this book means you're already on the right path, but humility forces me to declare that it might be only marginally deeper than Jon Stewart's book featuring naked pictures of historical figures.

The point is that you are not a bad person if you want to get some political news and opinions from TV. You may not even be a bad person if you turn on *The O'Reilly Factor* to play a drinking game where everyone drinks every time O'Reilly pretends to lose his temper, leers about a news item involving sexually loose women, or says something that's obviously a lie. (You are, however, on probation if you take O'Reilly seriously.) If you have a crush on Rachel Maddow or think *The Daily Show* has a pretty decent read on the political temperature, there's no reason to self-flagellate.

You don't need to turn off the TV—you just need to not live on a diet of TV alone. Luckily, the problem of people's living on TV alone is beginning to correct itself, though not with much help from the newspaper industry, which is currently dying from lack of advertising money. The Internet has gone a long way toward pushing people to read more, and more in-depth, about politics than they were just a few years ago. Even with video and audio available online, the easiest and most commonly accessed online content remains text. People read articles and blog posts to kill downtime at work, on their smartphones while waiting in line, and increasingly on their home computers in lieu of flipping on the TV (or, for a few multimedia addicts, while watching TV). Even better, the proliferation of blog commenting sections and online forums means that people cannot only read but also respond and have their own responses responded to, which pretty much forces all but the most stubborn to think a little harder about their opinions. (The stubbornly stupid to just hang out at the Free Republic.) It's a complete reversal of the passive, shallow responses that TV has encouraged for so long.

So what can you do to help? Well, not only read more books, but read more blogs and articles online, donate money to your favorite sources, and, most important, *leave comments.* Comments are like crack for people writing online content. Knowing that people are out there and engaging their ideas just pushes them to come up with more and deeper ideas. If we want the level of intellectual discourse to rise in this country, we need to reward the people providing it with the intellectual equivalent of giving them a cookie, which is giving them attention.

WHO GETS WHAT, WHEN:
Taxes and Public Wealth

CHAPTER THREE

I COME NOT TO BURY THE BUREACRAT,
but to Praise Her

Read enough right-wing literature or listen to enough right-wing radio, and you'll find that the most common villain, after favorites such as feminists, the homosexual agenda, college professors, and largely toothless congressional Democrats, is the nefarious race of paper-pushers known as "bureaucrats." In the shady world of the right-wing imagination, bureaucrats work tightly with liberals to create an ever-expanding government for the dual purpose of getting themselves the bestest and bestest-paying jobs in the whole world and, of course, emasculating conservative men. Searching for the word "bureaucrat" on conservative websites turns up a plethora of fear and loathing. *National Review* alone turns up some juicy bureaucrat hating:

> "But I've noted that bureaucrats don't think very highly of the judgment of the common citizen."

> "In the bit about health care, did you get Bush's Terrible Trifecta? Bureaucrats, trial lawyers and HMOs."

"Who the hell do these fool bureaucrats think they are, stealing my time like this?" (In reference to the census.)

"Bureaucrats trust process, not people."

And so on and so forth. In right-wing mythology, bureaucrats exist solely to make life hard for god-fearing, hardworking white men who merely want to make a couple dimes to rub together without having to worry about unimportant issues like paying their taxes or refraining from giving everyone in the neighborhood pollution-related cancer. Bureaucrats, unlike human beings, have no good motivations to offset their baser desires to obstruct for no good reason, be a pain in the ass, and cover their own asses. They certainly cannot be motivated to make the world a better place, because in the right-wing mythology, all human motivations are base and selfish. If a polluting businessman is base and selfish, surely the people trying to stop him are, right?

Powermongering bureaucrats who feast on human flesh have an extremely useful function. The specter of the evil bureaucrat is wielded to argue that "big government" shouldn't exist. Now, "big government" doesn't mean what you or I might think, which would be a government that's large in size and perhaps spends quite a bit of money. This can't be "big government," because under that definition, conservative Republicans *love* big government, since they're the ones who run up huge deficits and start extremely expensive wars to line the pockets of their corporate buddies. No, "big government" is government that spends your tax dollars improving the health and lives of everyday people. Thus, a million dollars to shoot a bomb into a wedding in a foreign country and kill all the attendees is "small government," but the same dollars spent on educating children or enforcing environmental regulations are "big government." The rule of thumb is that if you or anyone you know could conceivably benefit from a dollar of tax money, it's probably "big government." If the money kills someone or enriches someone that you'll never meet unless you're a servant, then it's "small government."

Bureaucrats are easy to demonize for the same reason that stoplights are easy to demonize: No one ever remembers all the thousands of times the stoplight turned green in quick order for them, even if that's 95 percent of their encounters with stoplights. When we hear the word "bureaucrat," we never think of the person who arranged for your college aid, who helped you get a government-subsidized loan, or who efficiently processed your tax refund. We think only of the time the IRS audited us. Bad memories just stick better. Even *Random House Dictionary* defines a bureaucrat using loaded, judgmental language: "1. an official of a bureaucracy. 2. an official who works by fixed routine without exercising intelligent judgment."

Interestingly, movement conservatism has done such a great job of demonizing bureaucrats in service of an ideological agenda that most people tend to forget, not only that bureaucrats also work in the private sector, but also that the vast majority of their unpleasant experiences with bureaucrats come from the private sector. Most of us have never dealt with an OSHA representative coming in and telling us that all the cooks in the kitchen must wear shoes to work, but we have sat waiting on the phone for hours to:

○ Get them to cancel our cell phone and accept that yes, we really did change service providers.

○ Figure out why our insurance company decided "broken leg" was a preexisting condition.

○ Get the cable company to commit to a narrower time period for a
service agent to show up than "any time between 8:00 AM Monday
and midnight Friday."

○ Have a manager at the bank reverse overdraft fees incurred because
they ran a check from someone else's account against your account.

I've spent many hours of my life hearing easy-listening versions of Madonna
hits from the '80s while on hold, but only a small fraction of that time was
given over to government bureaucracy. However, most people fail to make
this distinction. Such is the hate that bureaucrats generate in the human
heart—we don't even bother to distinguish between them. Conservatives are
able to whip people into a frenzy by telling them that universal health care
might mean long waits in the ER, piles of insurance paperwork, and bureau-
cratic wrangling over what doctor you can see, all without many people stopping to point out that this is the situation we currently have under a private
insurance system. The only way government bureaucrats could make it worse
would be by shoving pins under your fingernails while you fill out the fifth
page of paperwork asking for the same emergency contact information before
you're permitted to have a cast put on your broken arm.

But you can believe they wouldn't do that. Because while government
bureaucrats, like all bureaucrats, are more interested in their lunch breaks
and covering their own asses than in making your day any easier, they still
rate way below most private bureaucrats on the evilness scale, because private
bureaucrats work mostly for organizations that are trying to maximize their
own profits at the expense of your wallet. Government bureaucracies are set
up to protect the interests of the people. True, that means all the people,
not just a handful of rich people trying to get by with as much as they can,

so government bureaucrats will always be the enemy of the right. But even when they're putting you on hold or using a snippy tone with you, they work for you. Unlike, say, the bureaucrats at your local cable company or HMO.

But don't career bureaucrats give up trying to do a decent job, due to the lack of accountability that you hear so much about from Rush Limbaugh? The iconic right-wing image of the bureaucrat is that of a man using his time at work to run office betting pools or go over kitchen-remodeling plans—anything but actually doing his job. Surely what we need to do is introduce a level of accountability, perhaps by staffing management with political appointees instead of career bureaucrats?

Nope. As Shankar Vedantam reported in *The Washington Post* in November 2008, political scientist David E. Lewis reviewed the performance of political appointees versus career bureaucrats in similar positions and found that despite the political appointees' better education and resumes, the career bureaucrats did a better job. Managing a bureaucracy is an unglamorous, thankless job. Turns out, people who do it are willing to console themselves by being good at their jobs. Yes, bureaucrats console themselves. They also sleep eight hours a night, show up to happy hours in their tepid work outfits, own pets, and even have sex if there's nothing good on TV. They're people, like the rest of us.

I spent much of my twenties installed in one bureaucracy or another, working first in banking and then in financial aid at a university. It's true that you spend most of your time filing stuff and covering your ass. You learn how to tell people no and suffer their ire without breaking down, which could give others the impression that you've grown cold. But I did make the transition from being a private bureaucrat to a government one. And not just any government bureaucrat, but one working for a large federal program established as part of the Great Liberal Satan, LBJ's, Great Society, i.e., the most demonized of government bureaucracies. And I can tell you that the evil government-bureaucracy job bested the private-sector job in every way. I spent much of my time at the bank telling people who lived paycheck to paycheck that we just couldn't help them get ahead, or even relieve their growing debt load that wasn't helped by overdraft fees. I spent most of my time working in federal aid helping people realize their educational goals and their career dreams without sleeping on the street or stealing textbooks.

I also spent a lot of time planning lunch and sending email forwards to my friends. But I defy anyone who would claim these sorts of things are the unique sins of bureaucrats. I'd bet even the big-time editors of right-wing, bureaucrat-demonizing magazines have forwarded an lolcat in their time. "I'M IN UR BUROOCRACY DENYING UR CLAIM."

WE'RE ALL
SOCIALISTS.
And Capitalists.
Both. No, Really.

It took less than a week of partisan carping and Republicans popping up on cable news to shed crocodile tears over the dangers of socialism before the new president Barack Obama decided to hit the road and dominate the news cycle by selling the Democrats' economic stimulus package to the nation. The good news was that the bill was polling well, because Americans needed to believe that the government was doing *something* as our economy spiraled down the drain. The bad news was that the Republicans' bellyaching about socialism had traction at all, because they'd successfully confused the public about the nature of government, leading a large percentage of people to think that any new government spending on anything but defense must mean we'd wake up tomorrow as atheists, and another, larger percentage to at least fear and misinterpret government spending on social programs as the first step down the slippery socialism slide.

For people who managed to pass tenth-grade history class, the entire spectacle had the flavor of coming home to find your mom sitting on the floor, picking her nose, and feeding the boogers to the dog. We were, in other words, bewildered. Who were these people afraid that we were one stimulus bill away from replacing the stars and stripes with the hammer and sickle? Did they honestly think that FDR soothed the woes of a country mired in the Great Depression simply by giving invigorating fireside chats on the radio? No, my friends, FDR stuffed the American economy with social spending— job-creation programs, infrastructure building, aid to struggling families, and a popular pension program you might know as Social Security. It even has the word "social" in it! If that's not socialism, I don't know what is.

At some point in time, a nation that elected FDR four times and then turned out to hand New Dealer Lyndon Johnson a giant margin of victory turned into a nation that didn't understand that sometimes the government needs to spend money on social programs, and that doing so doesn't mean sacrificing our soul to Satan. How did it happen?

Historian and best-selling author Rick Perlstein, blogging at Our Future, explains what went on:

> *One answer, of course, is that the conservative move-ment* made it happen, *through sedulous political activism and skillful public propaganda. . . . Their secret weapon, across this span of decades, was racial resentment: the chain reaction, as Thomas and Mary Byrne Edsall put it in the most authoritative single volume on the subject, of "race, rights, and taxes," by which the white majority became convinced that when government got bigger it did so always at their expense, in the interests of enriching people of color.*

Decades of right-wing talk radio, whisper campaigns, Fox News, conservative think tanks and publications, and browbeating the mainstream media made "big government" a catchphrase that usually turned into the word "socialism" when tempers flared. To make the whole situation worse, all but a few liberals howling in the wilderness caved completely to this right-wing agitprop, including the luminaries of the Democratic Party. Bill Clinton notably shied away from being labeled a "big government" liberal by backing policies like free trade and slashing welfare—policies that were fiscally and morally questionable but nonetheless politically popular with grumpy white people. So, when Obama had to hit the road to defend an economic stimulus package totaling hundreds of billions of dollars, he faced a public that hadn't even heard in many decades the idea that government spending could be beneficial.

At the base of the nonargument that is screaming "big government!" or "socialism!" is the belief that any embrace whatsoever of nationalizing a sector of the economy or spending money on public welfare automatically makes a person a harsh anti-capitalist who is one beard and automatic weapon away from becoming the next Che Guevara. Liberals like to spend a lot of our time decrying black-and-white thinking, and the main reason is that we get called socialists for paying our taxes on time without complaining. That would make you sanctimonious about simplistic reasoning as well.

But I'm here to tell you that economic philosophy is not religion or marriage, which require you to pick one thing and stick with it. You can be a polyamorous cherry picker all you want with economics, and not only will you not be hypocritical or wrong, but you'll have the added advantage of being the only person in the room with common sense. Yes, you can be both a socialist and a capitalist.

In fact, socialists do this all the time in places that your right-wing relatives warn you not to travel to, such as France or some of those über-blond northern European countries. You don't need to know which ones, or even the particulars of their economy, to understand this, though you should probably learn about that stuff anyway so you can win pointless arguments with your family members or idiotic right-wingers online. Just understand: *You can live in those countries and own a private company that makes you money.* You can even incorporate and take investors!

They don't throw you in jail for being a rich son of a bitch in France, contrary to what you may have heard on your favorite AM gasbag talk-radio shows. If you stop and think about it for a moment, the French actually love rich people, because they are the main (possibly sole) source of cash flow into French-errific industries that sell things like mega-expensive wine and chocolates, high fashion, and French-countryside real estate. One could call these things symptoms of liberal elitism, but in reality it's just good old-fashioned expensive shit that only rich people can buy. And most rich people nowadays are capitalists, since being the landed gentry is so eighteenth century.

In all seriousness, pretty much every liberal slandered with the word "socialist" is actually a supporter of a mixed economy. That means some parts of the economy are nationalized, some parts are private but heavily intertwined with the government, and some parts are handled through capitalism, albeit well-regulated capitalism. I'm hoping readers who've lived through the recent economic crisis don't need an explanation for why a little regulation might help keep capitalist businessmen honest.

How do we decide which parts of the economy should be national-ized and which shouldn't? Through the disappointingly unideological means of assessing the situation pragmatically and asking if the profit motive in this economic sector or that leads to the best results for society, and if it doesn't, that sector becomes eligible for a reassessment to see if it needs to be nationalized. This is exactly how dreaded "socialist" nations, like Mexico and

Canada, settled on nationalized health care, for instance. The methodology isn't sexy, but, like many nonsexy things, it works.

But if socialism is like pregnancy—and there's no such thing as being a little bit socialist—then I have bad news for those who fear our slide into socialism: Friends, we're already there. Socialism is not just Social Security, it's also Medicare. Ironically, while Republicans have made ideologically motivated attempts to undermine both programs, they haven't gone far, because their avid, elderly, red-baiting base refuses to believe *their* socialism is socialism. But it's more than that. It's the roads you drive on and the schools your kids go to. You don't have to pay a fee to the fire department before it puts out a fire, which shows that we as a nation have already drifted away from our healthy, capitalist, free-market system and toward Satan worship. Ideologically, we've admitted that some sectors of the economy just work better if they're nationalized, which means that when we get whipped into a frenzy over fears of "big government," we're either hypocrites or incredibly stupid.

Truth is, except for a few goofballs on the left, we're all capitalists, even as we (whether we admit it or not) embrace certain kinds of socialism. Capitalism, especially if it's well regulated, does socialism one better in many economic sectors. I'm typing this on a MacBook Pro while listening to an iPod, two devices that exist only because Apple was a capitalist corporation that had to prove itself in a competitive market. As much as it pains me to admit it, conservatives aren't completely wrong when they point to the investment-competition-innovation cycle as one that can produce benefits for all of us. Too bad they fail to have the imagination—or the open eyes—to see that the public sector can reward creativity in other ways.

We're all socialists and we're all capitalists. It's a rare thing to have this much common ground. So many other political battles are fought on the either/or plain. You're either for or against abortion rights. You're either a believer or an atheist. You're either a batshit-crazy, warmongering terrorist fan or a peacenik hippie. So why on earth do Americans insist on fighting like cats and dogs over an issue that we actually all agree on? Are attention spans so short that we can't even take a moment to see that we're all socialist-capitalist mongrels?

"PRIVATIZATION"
Is Code for
"Steal the Public's Money"

On February 24, 2009, President Obama addressed the nation by calling a joint session of Congress in response to the economic crisis plaguing the country. It was a good speech. For Republicans, it no doubt felt like watching a manuscript they'd worked on for fifteen years being slowly fed into a fire, one page at a time, by someone who would then go on to fuck their spouse. Seventy-five percent of the anguish was strictly political—the pain of seeing the opposition put forth a masterful politician at the top of his game while your side has to rely on people who spend their weekends speaking in tongues and railing about black helicopters. Even the sleaziest, most opportunistic Republicans had to feel a pang of loss watching decades of anti-government crusading swirl down the toilet. Obama talked about government spending. A lot. On the people, not on tankers or on bombing other countries. And our desperate nation ate it up. It was almost as if we hadn't even heard the past decades of Republicans telling us to resent social spending and begrudge our neighbor every dime of job creation, health care, housing assistance, and food assistance. Watching a childish nation finally find its adult side must have pained Republicans who had given their lives to keeping us as childish as possible.

This, despite the fact that Obama hat-tipped a conservative fetish with a long pedigree: the concept of privatization. In reference to the job-creation aspects of the economic stimulus bill, Obama said, "Over the next two years, this plan will save or create 3.5 million jobs. More than 90 percent of these jobs will be in the private sector—jobs rebuilding our roads and bridges; constructing wind turbines and solar panels; laying broadband and expanding mass transit." In short, instead of creating a job corps under government management, the government would take bids from private contractors and hire them to do the job. This hat tip, designed to make more conservative voters comfortable, must have made the Republican guard clinch their asses especially hard in aggravation. On paper, it sounds like the privatization Republicans advertise as the solution to all problems. In reality, the stimulus package would take a commonsense approach that violated the Republican motto of never doing anything just because it makes sense.

Obama's mention referred to the more traditional intersection of tax money and the private sector. When a job needs doing, usually something with a definitive end date—building a bridge, teaching a roomful of high school students a one-day lesson about why drugs are bad (so they can ignore it)—setting up a permanent government position to do it makes no sense. So the government would take some bids from outside contractors, and ideally combine the highest quality for the lowest price to determine whom it hires. The bridge gets built or the teenagers get bored and hostile, the contractor gets fair compensation, and the taxpayer gets some value for her money.

At some point, a brilliant if small-souled conservative realized that by combining this sensible, apolitical system with ideological opposition to government bureaucracies, he could produce a brand-new way to filter wealth from people who work for paychecks to the already filthy-rich, exacerbating dangerous economic inequalities and, hopefully, restoring feudalism before we suffered complete economic collapse. This person's name is lost to history (or it's Grover Norquist—there's some debate about this), but the Bush administration embraced this stroke of evil brilliance wholeheartedly. No longer would it have to settle for pitifully low wages and regressive tax structures to encourage economic inequalities. Now it had a way to tax the poor and hand it directly to the rich through "privatization."

At its core, privatization takes the contract-job model and uses it to replace permanent government functions that operate more efficiently by hiring people directly to do the jobs. In other words, make everyone in the school, not just the people hired for occasional projects, private employees working for a profit-seeking business. Through a lot of hand waving, Republicans were able to distract the public from what should have been obvious, which was that this had to have been more expensive than just running the business yourself, for the same reason it's cheaper to scrub your own toilet than hire someone else to do it. When the government provides a service, it has two major expenses it has to cover: operating costs and people's salaries. If it's a private business, you have these expenses, plus you have to make a profit, which, if your money comes from the government, means it has to pay more so you have that, too.

The only real reason to do this is to take taxpayer money and give it to people in the private sector in return for reduced services per dollar spent, preferably in exchange for campaign donations. The excuse was that private businesses know how to run leaner than governments, because businesses are more likely to engage in open class warfare on their employees, slashing salaries and jobs as ruthlessly as possible. This makes some sense, in a dark sort of way, until you realize that labor costs are cut to increase profit, not charge the consumer—in this case, the government—less. Then it makes no sense at all. If we taxpayers spend money on something, it should at least provide decent-paying jobs we taxpayers can take.

Luckily for Republicans, they could float this idea in a media environment where most pundits feared analyzing even openly ludicrous claims, because doing so means Rush Limbaugh will write a parody song about you. So they set up a system to funnel all sorts of government money to friends. Charter schools, faith-based funding, and privatized prisons sprouted up like badly run, corner-cutting (for profit expansion) weeds. But nothing emboldened the schemers like the Iraq War, which allowed the worst sorts of taxpayer robbing to occur in conjunction with the use of "supporting the troops" as a catchall way to guilt anyone who looked too hard into looking away.

Of course, after the war dragged on for years, the patriotism-and–troop support distraction lost some of its bite. That's why there's a spitting chance you've heard the names Halliburton and Blackwater—two of the biggest companies in the new privatization system, and the basis of a Republican scheme to turn the largest entity that was considered to be under inviolate government control, the military, into a giant funnel directing your money to their rich friends. The Bush administration made sure to flaunt the "steal from the poor, give to the rich" aspects by offering these companies no-bid contracts, so they could charge whatever they wanted to offer services like shipping cheesecake around war zones under military protection. The soldiers protecting the Halliburton cheesecake went without armor unless they paid for it themselves, in case there was any doubt that the war was an experiment in using thin excuses to redirect taxpayer money to the rich.

Blackwater may have been even more disturbing, since there's been no attempt to paint it as anything but an extremely expensive mercenary service. Euphemisms like "private security" aren't even trying. A private army struck the Bush administration as a perfect storm of ideologically correct (if common sense—defying) ideas coming together. Outsourcing the military meant that the government could enrich its friends at taxpayers' expense, maintain a labor force without providing long-term benefits (though it did pay them exponentially higher salaries than real soldiers get), and evade basic human-rights laws and international treaties about legal warfare that were assumed to extend only to actual soldiers, not to mercenaries. Get rich while kicking the shit out of people without having to accept accountability—if they could throw in free blow jobs, it would be perfect. Frankly, I would not be shocked if history shows that was part of the deal. If you assume mercenaries aren't accountable to human-rights laws, why not assume that sex workers don't have to obey the law, because they're also private employees?

The Bushies got a little drunk on the power they had discovered to funnel taxpayer money into their friends' pockets, and, as with many a drunk person, there came a point when it stopped being fun to keep drinking and started being embarrassing. Winning the 2004 election seemed like permission to drink everything behind the bar. After that, they thought it would be awesome to drain everyone's Social Security accounts and give it to Wall Street with the empty promise that everyone would quadruple their money and, by the time the bottom fell out, be living fat and happy in Chile or something.

As far as schemes to make your rich friends richer go, it couldn't have been better. Dumping Social Security funds into the stock market would drive prices sky-high, and all the people in the market already— aforementioned rich fuckers—would see their values go through the roof. If they were wise to the scheme, they would then sell everything at the height of the market and sit around on their giant piles of gold, Scrooge McDuck—style. People stupid enough to think (because they live under rocks) that sort of artificial market inflation wouldn't eventually turn into a crash would be the ones left holding the bag when it happened. They, and everyone whose Social Security retirement savings had just gone up in smoke without their having an opportunity to stop it from happening.

The more paranoid among us would point out that the market crashed when markets generally do, in the last quarter of the year, and therefore wise observers would have realized that the Republicans ran a really strong chance of seeing a market crash in October 2008, right in time to hand the election to the Democrats. Sure, it could have happened in 2007 or 2009, but it was coming, and soon, due to the fact that the rising stock prices were built increasingly on bad mortgage investments and held together with spit. If I were a Republican and had known this was coming, I might have looked for schemes that would flood the market with cash to keep it up for a few more years, buying my party enough economic goodwill, based on lies, to get me through the 2008 election. Not that the Republicans were thinking this, but it is fascinating how Bush looked to raid the piggy bank for a stash of money that would just coincidentally do that.

Luckily for the nation and for Barack Obama's election prospects, Bush failed. People may not care much about Halliburton or mercenary firms, but if you grab their retirement savings and offer to bet it on a stock market that has seen both the dot-com bubble burst and the post-9/11 crash, they're going to tell you to fuck off—and perhaps suggest putting that money on a horse, as a better investment.

The common wisdom is that the economic crash really led to a shift in the political fortunes of Democrats and Republicans. That, and the country's impatience with the Iraq War. But the election of a Democratic majority in 2006 might have signaled that people were also done with the crazy idea that we can save money by wrapping it up in a bow and handing it over to rich people, so they can get richer while providing fewer services and even running off with our retirement savings.

THE RICH
Love Big Government
. . . for Themselves

By early spring 2009, the American public finally lost all hope of keeping track of how much money the federal government forked over to the very people who destroyed our economy by artificially inflating the housing market and then, when it crashed, revealing that they'd used bad mortgages to back up what started to seem to be the entire banking industry. Over and over again, from Democrats and Republicans, we heard that we needed to give the banks more of our money, lest our economy become even worse—and, by the way, everyone working in executive positions needed to keep making obscene amounts of money, despite the fact that they owed us for fucking us over so bad. Oh yeah, and an insurance company that gambled all its money away insuring bad investments that, as it turned out, it *knew* were shit also needed to be bailed out, to the tune of more money than most of us knew existed.

People were angry. Then they felt defeated, because there seemed to be no party willing to step up. Then they were angry again, because it seemed like the promise of democracy had finally been shown to be empty. They were screamingly angry, because while the banks faced one bailout after another, ordinary people who saw their jobs go up in smoke began to suspect they would never see a bailout, especially since we spent all the money on people who would probably just lend it to people who wanted to spend half a million dollars on homes worth a few grand.

But none of this was surprising.

What *was* surprising was how surprised many members of the mainstream media were that your average working American was fit to be tied over the mess. *Newsweek* epitomized this shock and fear when it put a picture of an angry mob on its cover in March, all with alarming language about populism. How could the average person not think the federal government existed, at least in its modern form, as anything but a giant funnel to channel people's money up to the richest members of society? Had they not lived through the past eight years of the Bush administration, which lived to find innovative ways to take your money and give it to the already wealthy?

Unfortunately, the Republican propaganda worked way too well in this case. The Republicans had sold themselves as the party of "small government" for so long—and had fashioned the Democrats as the "big government" party that wanted to take all the money and spread it around to the people—that people actually believed it. And because the Republicans showed dedication to withholding services that led to New Orleans washing away in a hurricane, they seemed to prove their stinginess, despite the fact that they had set up a pipeline of money to corporations like Halliburton. In fact, Democrats won because people who were desperate for help in the face of a failing economy wanted a taste of that big government.

But the truth of the matter is that no matter how much the very wealthy donated to the Republican Party and various libertarian and conservative think tanks to spread the message that they loathed "big government," it was never true, and the bank bailout proved it. Government spending has always been acceptable, as long as it lines the pockets of the people who feel they've earned it because they can cough up the enormous campaign donations to buy such favors. This was true under Republicans and it was true under Democrats, who worked together to rewrite bankruptcy laws to screw the little guy, secure outrageous copyright protections way past what the founders intended (including copyrighting genome codes!), provide no-bid contracts, and, eventually, bail out an entire financial industry that deliberately used fancy investment products to hide the fact that it was just making money up and pretending it existed. (This came to be known as "toxic assets"—mostly mortgage properties that were assumed to be worth often many times what they would actually fetch on the market.)

Not only that, but the willingness of supposed small-government fans to ban a government program depends entirely on whether or not rich people benefit from the service. Therefore, courts where corporations can settle disputes, highway systems necessary to make a ton of money, and, of course, the military—which can be used to protect American investments, as well as for war profiteering—will never be demonized by small-government shills. However, minor and underfunded agencies, such as OSHA, that were set up explicitly to monitor and prevent businesses who abuse employees and citizens were treated as the next step toward a fascist end of Western civilization itself. Any programs that offered aid directly to poor people also received the lion's share of abuse, no matter how small their relative budget was compared with untouchable items like national security.

After watching this problem with increasing dismay, though, I finally realized that there was one way in which the opposition to big government and the love of small government made sense. If you assume the adjectives "big" and "small" describe the size of the population that the government means to serve, then, yes, conservative, well-funded opposition to big government doesn't seem like a lie. A government for all 270 million–plus of us would be a big government, but conservative ideology supports a small government—in other words, a government that supports the interest of a small group of very wealthy people to exploit and screw over the rest of us. If most of us thought "big" described the number of dollars spent instead of the number of people served, then we were stupid for falling for such a transparent ploy.

Of course, the bailout inclines the public to believe that both Democrats and Republicans are for small government that spends big money on a small number of people who don't have enough space in their small hearts to care about the big number of Americans left out in the cold. Partisans would probably call this unfair, because the bank bailout was intended to keep all of us from going broke, due to the fact that if the banks blinked out of existence, they'd take all our deposits with them. But the government's willingness to play ball with rich bankers to save them from the mistakes they made, while the rest of the country pays the price, doesn't speak well for the strategy.

CONSCIOUSNESS RAISING ISN'T JUST FOR Identity Politics

———— 66 ! 99 ————

We have the second wave of feminism to thank for the concept of consciousness raising, a term that has more than a whiff of political mumbo-jumbo but actually refers to a simple concept. Feminists realized that a major obstacle to pushing women to fight sexism is that women, who'd been raised in a sexist system, might not initially know how to identify sexism well enough to fight it. It's like air and sunshine—until you take a step back and really pay attention to it, you forget it's even there. Of course, air and sunshine aren't much like sexism, in that they're generally good things. The good news is that the consciousness raising that needs to be done to promote people's investment in the public wealth is more like pointing out the air and the sun than pointing out the pervasive problem of sexism.

People fall for right-wing-government bashing because they don't see all the various services that government provides for them. They may have a surface understanding that the roads, courts, schools, cleanish air, clean food, dropping smoking rates, fire departments, grandparents' health care, postal services, scientific research, regulated markets, safe work environments, forty-hour workweeks, Social Security checks, Internet access, libraries, low crime rates, lack of foreign invaders, and right to call the cops when their neighbors are throwing a loud party are examples of the things that government does for them, but the high levels of service we've come to expect are invisible to us because they work. Good government, like good waiters, does its job efficiently and without overly distracting you by grinning and telling corny jokes and interrupting your conversation with your actual companions. The downside is that you might forget how hard the government works for you if it's not in your face, begging for a tip.

To make it worse, the generally competent, if not always super-fun-awesome functions, of the government mean that people remember only the horror stories, because exceptions tend to stand out and stick in your mind. You don't remember the thousands of letters and packages you've sent and received that got to their destination on time, but you do remember that one time a letter got lost fifteen years ago. That, coupled with an endless stream of ideological wankery pouring from right-wing media, makes it really easy for people to fall into the trap of believing that the government doesn't serve much of a legitimate purpose, and that it taxes you only out of sheer assholery.

The only cure for all the stupid, misleading right-wing–speak is positive, truth-based counterarguments to raise people's consciousness of how much the government already does for them, so they realize that they ask for more without worrying too much about its all going to hell.

There are two major tactics you can take. First, you can simply point out the air and the sun—or, in this case, the fire department and your Social Security checks. This strategy is particularly fun to use against maddening libertarians who believe, as 99 percent do, that they're much smarter than they really are. Just beware that libertarians, when asked how they'd put out fires on their houses without the fire department, try to change the subject most of the time, or they toss red herrings everywhere. Be patient and continue asking them if they'd really like to see all the above services disappear—or how private companies could really be expected to fund public education or fire departments for everyone—until they can't avoid the question any longer.

The other one may be even more fun. For people with legitimate concerns about the horrors of bureaucracy, it helps tremendously to remember that private corporations also employ complex, maddening bureaucracies that often work much less than government bureaucracies, because they have a profit interest in getting complainers off the phone. This is doubly true of any corporation that has a contract with you, which means it benefits if it "forgets" or stonewalls your attempts to terminate.

When right-wingers trot out bureaucracy fears, I reply by simply agreeing that bureaucracy is hell and trotting out my endless stories about my tangles with corporate bureaucracies, which beat any tangles with government bureaucracy in both volume and levels of hold music–based horror. Like the three weeks of constant phone calls it took to get the credit agency to accept that I really had paid off an outstanding debt. Or my multiweek battle to get a satellite dish properly installed. I couldn't even call the customer service line for my Roomba without having to spend 15 minutes on hold, all to get them to tell me I needed to change a filter. The DMV looks like a model of efficiency compared to this. Or I just bring up a horror story about trying to get an insurance company to pay for a medical treatment that it promised to pay for.

A little experience with the intersection of government and corporate bureaucracies always helps. For me, working as a financial-aid officer at a major university for a time meant that I had to help students get not only government-funded/-run scholarships, grants, and loans but also secure private loans. The vast difference between the two would make any reasonable person write thank-you letters to LBJ's corpse for setting up student financial aid, since the first category usually required two to three keystrokes per student to get them their money, while the latter category often meant weeks of my sitting on the

phone with bank representatives to untangle the bureau-
cratic nightmares that corporations set up to make sure
they don't leak a single penny of profit to some undeserv-
ing mere customer. Of course, not everyone benefits from
this level of experience in the intersection of the two, but
I offer up the example to jog your memory and help you
come up with your own contrasting examples.

"!"

BECAUSE EVERYONE

Gets Sick at Some Point:

Health Care

CHAPTER FOUR

FREE MARKET HEALTH CARE
Is Writing a Check for the Pleasure of Being Told *to Fuck Off*

Watching the public debates about universal health care that have been happening on and off since the early '90s can feel at times like you've fallen through the rabbit hole into a land where ordinary human logic doesn't function. Most people find the entire debate hopelessly complicated, and I suspect the right wing wants it to be that way, because if you tried to make it simple, you'd find yourself facing a simple question.

Given a choice between a system where every dollar paid in comes out in the form of health care (and some off-the-top money to manage the system) and a system where every dollar that goes in is considered potential profit that should be wrested from being returned as health care, which system would you choose as the one that will pay for your health care? Think carefully. The one that is set up to give you health care, or the one set up to deny you care in hopes of making a profit? You can put the book down and take a walk to clear your head, if you need to. This question lies at the center of the debate, so you should probably have a pretty good handle on what you think the answer will be before you dive in.

Back? Good. I suspect that you chose the system where you get the health care, instead of having to fight an insurance company that was set up to make shareholders rich more than to keep you alive and healthy. Unless your brain has been completely fried by the heavy use of the word "socialist" in the right-wing media, the beautiful simplicity of the situation should impress you.

If you think about it, for-profit health insurance belongs in the same category as beauty pageants, mullets, and heavy-metal power ballads— things that shouldn't exist by any logical measure and would completely confuse someone from an alien culture trying to make sense of ours. It makes less sense to have a taxpayer-provided police force, since you probably have more of an ability to get a gun and defend yourself than you do to get a medical degree to treat your own illness. A gun costs less than using medical facilities does, too. Plus, most of us get mugged or assaulted fewer times than we go to the doctor, making the police department seem like a luxury next to health care.

But we value the public peace, and so we pony up for a police force, realizing it's probably worth the taxes we pay not to have criminal gangs conducting shootouts on our lawns. Since the chance that you'll need reliable health care at some point in your life approaches 100 percent, perhaps having peace of mind knowing that's on hand will also be worth it to you.

Private insurance absolutely doesn't want to pay for your health care with perfectly good money that could go toward buying its executives bigger yachts. This is where I should mention that Michael Moore made these points in the movie *Sicko,* which was discredited in the mainstream media because he took actual pictures of Cuba and showed that, contrary to the claims of American propaganda, the sun does shine there and people play cards and walk on two feet. If he'll tell lies like that, who knows what other lies he'll tell? Surely all those people he lined up who found out that just

because they had insurance didn't mean they had health care had to be fig-
ments of his imagination, right?

Still, he had a point. If insurance companies pay for your health care, then
they do have less money for themselves, and that's got to bug their management.
It would be weirder if they didn't put a great deal of effort into denying people's
claims, refusing to cover people with preexisting conditions unless those people
pay unaffordable insurance premiums up front, and hunting around to discover
preexisting conditions when people filed claims so they could dump those folks
and take their money. If they actually put the customers ahead of profit, that
would go against the very grain of capitalism, and next thing you know, we'd
all have pictures of Fidel Castro on our walls. So, for god and apple pie, they
have to tell you to fuck off when you file a claim.

Don't take Moore's word for it. I got dumped by one insurance company because I had a bad Pap smear—the company claimed this indicated
I had a preexisting condition that I should have known about and dumped
me. I didn't have cervical cancer, but if I had, at this point I would have
been fucked more by the expense than by the cancer. Luckily, I was able to
get another company to sign me on, despite this preexisting condition, and
I do my best to avoid having to use health care and get its attention as one
of those dangerous people who wants health care coverage just because she
pays for it. Imagine the disaster facing anyone who doesn't have a clean bill
of health like I do.

Or don't, because there are plenty of examples of people in the worst
circumstances. The mainstream media dumped on Moore for covering
middle-class people who follow all the rules but get screwed by the insurance company and then guiltily started to cover the same stories. In April
2009, for instance, *The New York Times* reported on the Walkers, a Texas couple whose son had testicular cancer in high school and whom they couldn't

insure, especially after the mother lost her job because of the failing economy. The sword of Damocles hangs over the heads of people like this, since cancer can come back, and the Walkers know that it cost more than $2 million the first time around. If they can't afford to pay for insurance, they sure as hell can't pay that. This is standard operating procedure under the free market health care model, though.

How did we get into this horrible situation? Insurance companies were meant to insure for relatively rare situations, which made getting their money back much easier. Most of us don't see our cars get stolen or face disastrous injuries at work that prevent us from returning, two situations in which paying an insurance company just in case the worst happens makes sense. The companies are betting you don't need them, and you're hoping you don't. It's not a perfect situation, but in a grubby capitalist society where everyone's out to make a buck off everyone else's back, it's not bad.

Health care used to be pretty rare, back when the prescription for asthma was to move to Arizona and the prescription for heart disease was to cut back on salt and pray. Insurance companies may have had reason to believe that they wouldn't have to pay out enormous amounts of money to keep people alive and healthy in those days. The levels of medical intervention to keep people alive and healthy have grown exponentially in the past few decades, which we should consider an unmitigated good, but unfortunately, it's made paying for health care through the free market nearly impossible. Now the people who make it through their entire lives without requiring expensive medical care compromise the tiny minority. In insurance terms, it's as if 99 percent of customers routinely get cars stolen or require workers' compensation.

You'd think insurance companies would almost be happy to just give up the ghost and let the government pay them a nominal fee to stop doing business and go away, and not lobby endlessly to keep single-payer health care a political impossibility. But, alas, big companies don't work according to real human logic. Bookies who discover that gamblers all bet on events that absolutely will happen close up shop and move to greener pastures, but once you move into the official position of a corporate bigwig, admitting defeat apparently becomes impossible, and you will fight for your broken industry as if it were the last blow job on Earth.

Which means that Americans will be stuck with this system, even with legal reforms that squash preexisting-condition clauses and offer public options as alternatives. No Democrat dares challenge the monolithic insurance industry by proposing national health insurance, like Medicaid, for all. Clearly, we have no choice as a country but to all develop horrible, expensive diseases until we completely bankrupt the insurance industry and it has no choice but to give up. Perhaps the new expression of patriotism will be to pick up smoking in the name of attacking the insurance industry, one pair of diseased lungs at a time.

PAY FOR YOUR NEIGHBOR'S
Ounce of Prevention
(and Save Yourself a Pound of Cure)

One of the head-slapping, deaf-to-irony issues as conservatives and liberals debate universal health care is that of prevention. Liberals argue that universal health care will improve preventive care. But conservatives argue that they don't want to pay for the health care costs of people who refuse to engage in prevention. Of course, what they do by arguing this is ignore the fact that the current health care system actively discourages preventive health care.

How? Simple. Your insurance company assumes that it doesn't have you for life. Odds are, by the time you get old and develop a whole bunch of health problems, you'll be some other insurance company's problem. Even more likely, you'll be the government's problem because you'll be on Medicare by then. So while objectively it costs less for you to get your regular checkups now and catch any problems early, it means your insurance company has to pay money now to save someone else money later. For them, it's like putting $200 in a savings account with 10 percent interest that only someone else can access. From a business perspective, paying for prevention is madness, and your co-pays for routine checkups reflect this.

So when conservatives raise a fuss about how much universal health care will cost us, feel free to call bullshit. Not having universal health care is already costing us a fortune, because we get to pay for people's lifetime of avoiding routine prevention when they get passed from having private insurance (or no insurance) into the Medicare system. Which you pay for. If you have your doubts about this, check your next pay stub. The government kindly breaks it down for you.

Sadly, the chance of our seeing a single-payer system within the next couple of decades is slimmer than the chance that another *Spider-Man* sequel will become a critical hit. It's sad, because you can't do better than that for incentivizing preventive care, since you will definitely be on the same insurance plan when you're young and spry as when you're old and the years of living start to catch up with you. So every $200 insurance companies toss in the account is theirs to withdraw. Once you add even one or two competitors in there, you just encourage everyone in the system to sell you short on the preventive care you need, and then punt you to someone else when you get sick.

You really see the difference when you go to a place like England, which has national health services. Last time I went there, everywhere I turned I saw signs encouraging people who want to stop smoking to pop into one of the thousands of clinics all over the country that offer free services to help you quit. Good luck finding something like that in the United States. Oh, sure, you get plenty of public service announcements warning you about the dangers of smoking while ignoring the fact that people who want to quit don't have a lot of resources. And there are plenty of for-profit companies that will sell you gum, patches, or kits to help quit, for a price. But there's no one who'll help you quit for free, because there's nothing in it for them. However, if an institution knows that paying $5,000 to help you quit now will save it

$5 million down the road as it strains to save you from lung cancer or emphysema, then it has every reason to spend that money.

Of course, we could save all this money altogether by putting people down like they're horses with broken legs the second they get sick. But that neat and clean solution tends to go against the self-interest of all of us, rich or poor, because all but a few of us will find ourselves in a situation one day where we need expensive health care to survive. The "put people down" strategy would have what we sharp political minds call very little traction with the public, despite its obvious money-saving benefits.

UNIVERSAL HEALTH CARE
and Putting the
Farmers' Market Near You

Decades of fighting over health care reform have hardened the discourse about it into, for most people, a series of slogans. "Socialized medicine!" "Single payer!" "Waiting lists!" "Price controls!" Part of the reason is that most people don't have the attention span to focus on policy wonks' wonking about the endless array of options, but mostly, the debate hardened because that's what debates do after decades of people's talking a lot without anything happening. Conservatives have recurring nightmares about a mandatory hammer and sickle adorning every doctor's office, and liberals have reduced their dreams to imagining that they go to the hospital, get care, pay a reasonable or even nonexistent fee, and never have to get caught up haggling with an insurance company that denies their claim on the grounds that while having a two-foot crowbar sticking out of your abdomen may be uncomfortable, the company doesn't recognize anything under six feet as a medical emergency.

Dramatically reduced expectations will pay out in meager dividends. As I write this, the debate over health care reform is just heating up, and if we're lucky, by the time this book comes out, we'll have some dramatically watered-down version of something that might look like health care reform if you squint at it sideways while hopping on one foot. If the option to buy government-run health insurance remains, I'll be hard to reach for book readings, because I'll be running through the fields, delirious with joy that something finally went halfway right for once.

Digression aside, the point of this is to plead with you to start asking for more from government health care plans, and not let conservative paranoia artificially set your standards below commonsense levels. There's just so much that the government can do for health care besides only providing everyone with affordable insurance that will actually cover your medical bills. Health care reform could do things like put a farmers' market near your house, with all sorts of nice walking or bike paths between you and that market so you can get some exercise while going to get that healthful produce.

How? Well, as I noted before, you can do a lot when you make prevention a major part of your health care reform package. It's not just about creating free programs to help quit smoking, or paying doctors' bonuses if they prove they've gotten patients to quit smoking, take up an exercise program, or adopt a healthier diet. Once the government starts really getting into the idea that prevention saves it money in the long term, all sorts of goodies that liberals have been demanding forever can get funding through health care, because these reforms really do make people healthier.

Take pollution reduction. Right now, the biggest battle is between environmentalists and conservatives who, for ideological/assholish reasons or because they've been paid off by the oil companies, resist any suggestion that perhaps Americans would be better off if we drove less and saw the blue sky without a haze in it anymore. Realistically, environmentalists have a better case, but since each side has one argument, most Americans call it a draw and let the drive-everywhere status quo stand.

But if you bring health care into the debate, things change dramatically. Liberals can point out that the car culture leads to sedentary lifestyles that lead to long-term health damage like heart disease and diabetes, which costs us money. So if we got people out of their cars and onto their feet or bicycles, we wouldn't just be doing a good deed, we'd be saving money. Buy a sidewalk now to avoid paying for a quadruple bypass later. And did we mention that it's not exactly good for lifetime health prospects if you're inhaling pollution day in and day out?

The fantasy of an accessible, affordable farmers' market can totally fit into health care reform. Right now, the government's agriculture subsidies have all been written without paying much attention to people's health needs. That means, if I may channel Michael Pollan for a moment, tons of subsidies that end up making the dollar menu at McDonald's possible but don't do a whole lot toward getting you near a diet that might allow you to take a shit more than once a month. But if preventing colon cancer becomes not just a good deed, but a way to save money? We've got a little more political will to move agriculture subsidies from the meat industry to making more fresh produce available.

Okay, the farmers' market might be the pipe dream in this, but if you don't aim high, you won't get anything. So I'm taking the noncynical position of saying, "Why not?" If we can get the political will to change up decades' worth of ingrained agricultural-subsidy structures, then why not direct some of the brand-new subsidies to small farmers who bring bushels of fresh, ripe vegetables to the park, where you can stroll around in the sunshine, perhaps while laughing joyously amidst the glow of new love, while humble farmers handpick their favorite items so you can make a romantic dinner for. . . .

Well, like I said, if you don't ask for the moon, you won't even get a decorative plate commemorating the moon landing.

YOU CAN
DO MORE THAN
Cross Your Fingers and Hope
You Don't Get Sick

—— 66 ! 99 ——

More than any topic in this book, health care—in terms of both my arguments and my action items—makes for the biggest guessing game. While I'm writing this, congressional committees are writing competing bills to reform health care, Republicans are trying to tell the public that they're going to enslave your family doctor, and pundits are running around saying inane things like, "Will debates over abortion coverage be the end of health care reform?" But I have a strong sense, based on my ability to read and not forget what I read immediately, that we won't see the kind of health care bill that we really deserve at the end of this process, and that in fact, the battle may have just begun.

As you hold this book in your hands, there's a strong possibility that we've got a universal health care bill of some sort. If you didn't have insurance before, you may even have it now. If so, congratulations! I'm glad you can go to a doctor without being on death's door. You probably also noticed that the health insurance you've got is not single payer, which may surprise you, since you were subjected to months of Republicans' screaming, "Socialism!" That may have led you to believe that we would be getting something in the ballpark of socialism, such as a single-payer system like the U.K. has, where you go to a doctor and pay them in signatures and smiles. You may realize that you're still paying insurance premiums and co-pays. At least your insurance company didn't dump you when you revealed your evil intentions to overreach by getting routine cancer screening your carrier didn't want to pay for. But things haven't changed as much as you thought they would.

You've therefore got the classic symptoms of someone who realizes that we've come a long way, but we have a long way to go.

Of course, all my high hopes might be for nothing, because it's just as likely that congressional Democrats failed you utterly. And that you spent your money on this book because you needed something to distract you while you die slowly from that exotic infection you got walking barefoot through your kitchen, which you thought was safe, though it turns out that you need full-body protection against your own food, because a couple decades of deregulation frenzy mean no one stopped the manufacturer from selling you food it knew had been contaminated with an exotic infection. Nor did you realize your insurance company, high on defeating health care reform, has decided that walking around your house without shoes is a pre-existing condition. And the money it will take to save your life would buy you at least fifty thousand copies of this book, but you can't afford that, so you'll just buy the one and hope that you can forget the pain for a little while longer.

In which case you see that we're at square one and more action is needed.

In all honesty, contacting your representatives is probably the most important thing you can do on this issue. They get besieged by lobbyists for insurance companies to the extent that they think all human beings in the whole world that have any needs or opinions are insurance company lobbyists, and your input might remind them that they have constituents that elected them who might one day get exotic infections. Picking up the phone and calling is the best idea. Sending a letter or an email also works, but make sure you write it yourself and send it directly from your own home or email account. Try to avoid using the form letters on websites like MoveOn, because many politicians have filters to block them.

And if you have a representative who won by being the biggest, craziest wingnut of them all, then find someone in a leadership position, perhaps on a committee that writes health care legislation, and just target that person with phone calls and letters. Or do that anyway, because politicians, like dogs, tend to respond most strongly to attention.

"!" TOILET, MEET MONEY: The War on Drugs

CHAPTER FIVE

ME? DRUGS? NEVER.
I Get High on Opinions.

Observers of American hypocrisy had a great month in January 2009, and not just because not-at-all-gay Ted Haggard was doing the talk-show circuit with his wife to explain that his habit of smoking meth and topping gay hookers should in no way, shape, or form lead an audience to assume that he was anything less than 100 percent, all-beef-patty heterosexual. No, we hypocrisy addicts had seconds with the phony national crisis over the revelation that the Olympic gold-medalist swimmer Michael Phelps had smoked pot.

You read that right. He smoked pot. Many of us anxiously waited for further shocking revelations. Perhaps Phelps, in his depraved past, had committed other grievous moral errors, such as jaywalking, breaking a New Year's resolution to get up before 10:00 AM even on weekends, or forgetting to rewind a video before returning it to the video store. The pearl-clutching hypocrisy started immediately, with Elizabeth Hasselbeck of *The View* squealing about what a horrible person Phelps must be to smoke pot, until Whoopi Goldberg hit her bullshit limit and told Hasselbeck to step off.

Finger-wagging letters were sent by the Olympic Committee and people writing to newspaper editors, complete with the twenty-first-century version of claiming you'll pray for someone, which is to suggest that your target has mental issues that should be addressed through therapy. It was hard to tell if the problem was that Phelps had smoked pot at all, or that he'd been caught on camera, which only led to the suspicion that, in America, getting caught is the real crime. All this hysteria over behavior that most people are certain is relatively harmless, because they've done it and probably still do it. Yes, even you, dear reader, have probably not only lifted the joint but also inhaled.

After Bill Clinton made his famous statement about smoking marijuana, a million stupid jokes from people bravely admitting they'd inhaled cropped up, and every single time, I rolled my eyes because, realistically speaking, admitting you've inhaled in this country should be as brave as admitting that you've jaywalked. (By the way, jokers, thanks for the eye strain.) I don't think I know anyone above the age of fourteen who hasn't smoked pot at some point in time. I've smoked pot, though I generally try to refrain because I've smoked enough to realize that, on second thought, I don't like it and far prefer the far more dangerous hobby of drinking. But even writing these sentences fills me with dread, because, like most Americans, I've completely absorbed the taboo against admitting drug use in a public forum. Half the reason I'll even admit to having smoked pot is that I don't do it anymore, so I get the free pass that we extend to repentants, even though I'm actually not repentant.

We all get it. We've all done it, and it's fun to talk about at parties. (I regale my comrades with stories of seeing marijuana gardens during my childhood in West Texas, where pot flows more freely than water.) But to admit to drug use, even something as harmless as pot smoking, is to risk your entire economic and social future. How will you get a job if potential employers (who've all smoked pot) find out? How will you face your future children (who will smoke pot) if you admit you've done it? How will you have a future in politics if the voters (many of whom are high as they vote) find out? The list goes on.

The problem with the current system, in which everyone does it and everyone pretends they don't, is that every day we play at this game is a day we flush money down the toilet otherwise known as the War on Drugs. Few people really enjoy flushing $40 billion a year trying to stop an unstoppable problem, and most of us realize that the percentage of that going toward fighting marijuana use in particular is like waging a very expensive war against caffeine. But speaking up against the War on Drugs in an atmosphere where everyone has or does use illegal drugs but won't admit it is as good as hanging a sign on yourself that says Dope Fiend.

You see this playing out in the battle over medical marijuana. The assumption is that the majority of people fighting for it are pot smokers who want to take steps toward legalization, which makes them a joke at best, but definitely suspect in the eyes of the public that also smokes pot and would benefit from legalization. It's like a giant witch hunt targeting people who have hair for wanting hairbrushes legalized. Of course they're self-interested! They're also right, and they want to help you out.

Of course, part of the fear that keeps people mum on the topic is the fear that speaking out about drug laws will make them targets for police persecution in a state where cops have been caught planting drugs. Which doesn't make it seem like Americans are living in a communist dictatorship at all. I have no idea how real this threat is, but I suspect the fear of it drives some of the paranoia, though most of it has to do with the taboo of admitting to unrepentant drug use. An analogous situation is the abortion debate—

many pro-choice activists have had abortions, I'm sure, but few will speak about them for fear of being tarred by the very stereotypes they combat.

We as a nation need to speak up—and now—about the issue. The War on Drugs wastes money and law-enforcement time without really addressing the problem, has wreaked havoc on many developing countries that are subject to criminal gangs, and appears to exist, as I'll argue, for the sole reason of propping up a racist prison industrial complex. Neither Democrats nor Republicans seem inclined to give an inch on the issue, because they feel no pressure from the public. And that's because we're all so scared of being labeled potheads that we fail to remember that the people doing the labeling are going home and smoking up, too.

THE PERMANENT
Nonvoting Underclass

It's a rough day when a young liberal puts together these two disturbing facts:

○ The War on Drugs, and on crime in general, escalated dramatically after the Civil Rights movement made black-voter enfranchisement a physical as well as a theoretical reality.

○ Two percent of the nation as a whole, but 13 percent of black men, have lost the right to vote, due to state laws that ban felons from doing so.

It's the day when you begin to wonder if this might all be a coincidence, or if there's some kind of crazy conspiracy going on. Don't even think about the fact that these numbers aren't really that small, when you consider the small margins that decide so many elections. Bush won the 2004 election with a margin of about three million people, but nearly five million potential voters have been disenfranchised because of laws that strip felons of the right to vote.

When this happens to you—and it may as you read this book—take a few breaths and relax. This is a good moment for a political education in getting past the false dichotomies that people latch on to far too often in our political system. It's neither a crazy coincidence nor a conspiracy. Like many things in our country, it's a system that evolved due to many choices made by people who were motivated, depending on where they fell on the political spectrum, by either gross racism/classism or cowardice in the face of campaign commercials telling voters they aren't tough on crime. (I'll leave it to you, discerning reader, to figure out which group belongs to which political party.) Now that it benefits Republicans and has been considered politically toxic for Democrats, there's not much hope of changing it.

But you should want to all the same. Sadly, the partisan agreement on this issue leads many liberals to give up even trying to form opinions or care about felon-disenfranchisement laws, or about the drug war that means that we have the world record for lengthy incarceration. Really, drug laws are an authoritarian's wet dream. You have a behavior that's, let's face it, socially acceptable and widespread, though it's considered shameful and is rarely talked about. Therefore, you can selectively enforce bans, because, hey, you can't get them all, right? And with that, you can create a permanent underclass.

The only way it could have worked out better for authoritarians would have been if they had banned masturbation. And don't laugh—if you've spent any time talking to the "pro-life" contingent of the conservative movement, you'll find that banning masturbation hasn't been taken off the table.

Of course, the drug war doesn't just turn huge percentages of otherwise eligible, hostile-to-Republican voters into nonvoters. It doesn't even do only that while also getting everyone with similar names onto purge rolls to keep them from voting as well. It does all this and puts another obstacle in the way of drug-using lower-class people who want to claw their way up the economic ladder to where they can compete with drug-using but largely unpunished privileged people. As if there weren't enough.

Unless you work for yourself, you're probably going to face a criminal-background check when you apply for a job. And if you're low on the food chain, you're facing piss tests to make sure you don't use drugs. Good luck getting a job if you fail either of these tests, unless the job is a go-nowhere position that barely pays—and frankly, in this economy, getting even that might be a stretch.

But, you may be thinking, the key to moving up the food chain is getting one of those shiny college degrees within the reach of everyone who can scrape together the grades, the time, and the ability to fill out an application for federal student aid. But even the holy grail of higher education has been contaminated by drug-war paranoia. If a student gets a drug conviction while receiving aid, she's cut off from receiving more, unless she finishes a rehabilitation program. That's fine for students who don't need to work through school and have the time for that, or whose parents have enough money that federal aid is irrelevant. For the people trying to punch up out of poverty, however, it's another giant "fuck you."

Hey, far be it from me to say that our drug war sends the message that drugs are the playthings of the wealthy. It's not yacht or BMW ownership; it's still technically, and occasionally actually, illegal for rich people to use or sell drugs. But somehow our system has evolved into an authoritarian dream in which the rich and poor alike smoke dope, but the poor actually have to contend with that permanent record you hear so many jokes about.

FIGHTING ON THE LOCAL LEVEL

66 ! 99

Unfortunately, when it comes to pushing back against the War on Drugs, many dissenters think it's enough to suck really hard on a joint and feel the warm, if sedating, surge of rebellion against the Man. And then watch a silly cult comedy. But I shouldn't be so hard on the stoners. One could and should make many jokes about how stoners, who have remarkable abilities to turn a vast array of household objects into smoking devices, have a collective energy and creativity that could solve any problem, if they cared to. On the other hand, when it comes to pushing back against the War On Drugs, the stoner crowd has devised a not-bad strategy of starting on the local level.

Ballot initiatives about medical marijuana have exploded in the past decade as a way to reveal the absurdity and cruelty of the War On Drugs, and to motivate people on a local level to start admitting that they don't actually care that much if their neighbors use drugs responsibly, i.e., use while not breaking other laws that actually matter to their neighbors. At the county and state levels, stoners have achieved remarkable success with this strategy, despite the major obstacles against them. Smelling strongly of patchouli tends to turn people against your message, even if you were selling calorie-free chocolate.

That level of success despite obstacles should attract notice. Part of what's worked is that the stoners wisely chose a series of poster children for the cause—people who didn't fit the profile of a pot smoker, and may have never even smoked pot before, but faced horrible, chronic pain that only smoking pot helped alleviate. The lesson is that bringing the non-patchouli crowd into the cause helps. And if you're a member of the non-patchouli crowd, then step up and speak up.

The straighter the spokespeople against the War on Drugs are, and the more they target their immediate community, the better they do. They drive home the point that the War on Drugs isn't about purging our communities of a few ne'er-do-wells; it's about ripping our communities apart at the seams, criminalizing behavior that tends to fall in the categories of harmless partying, experimentation, or addiction but isn't generally malicious or even unusual.

These spokespeople also emphasize that you don't have to be a user or a derelict to see that the War on Drugs is a waste of time and money that has become intractable, in no small part because it serves racist and classist ends. It shouldn't matter who's giving the message if the message is good, but when it comes to politics, them's the breaks. And if you look sharp in a suit, you might want to consider employing that talent to speak up on behalf of those who don't.

IN THE BEDROOM:
Reproductive Rights and Access

CHAPTER SIX

ONLY ONE SIDE OF THE
Abortion Debate
Wants You to Get Laid

If you asked a reproductive-rights advocate like me about the single most frustrating aspect of the abortion debate, you probably wouldn't get an answer about sanctimonious right-wing nuts or the fight's endless, unwieldy nature, though both of these aspects often make having your fingernails pulled out by pliers look pleasant in comparison. No, it's that the public just doesn't get it. And by "it," I mean what the fight is really about.

Your average member of the public sees the fight like this:

Corner #1: Pro-lifers. Judged by the average member of the public on a scale from sympathetic people who feel deep devotion to their cause to simpering morons who kind of worship fetuses. What's not in doubt is their commitment to fetal life, which the public assumes they consider precious beyond belief.

Corner #2: Pro-choicers. These are the feminists, who are assumed to be, depending on whom you talk to, anyone from whip-cracking, cold-hearted bitches with no maternal instinct to sympathetic figures who genuinely think that while abortion is never easy, it should be safe because it's not going away.

Because the legal battle laid out in *Roe v. Wade* (now officially the most famous Supreme Court decision in history—score one for slutty feminists!) weighed state interests in fetal life against a woman's right to privacy, the public at large falsely assumes the political battle over abortion is over fetal rights versus women's rights.

Certainly, pro-lifers go out of their way to front like they're just Team Fetus in this battle. Even the most avid sports fans have to envy the way pro-lifers drench themselves in their mascot's imagery. I've seen fetus dolls, fetal-feet necklaces, checks with fetuses printed on them, and, of course, fetus T-shirts and bumper stickers. In addition to which, no matter how much it makes people hate them, they can't quit waving pictures of bloody fetuses at you, as if they're sure that this will be the time you'll warm up to the images as quickly as they did. They would very much like you to believe that they're in this only because they want to make sure that abortion goes away forever, by any means necessary.

It's also becoming increasingly important to the pro-lifers to make sure that you really don't think they're just misogynists who have a problem with female sexuality. They like women! They like women so much that they want every woman to experience the joys of motherhood on a regular basis, whether she likes it or not. With this goal in mind, Team Fetus has started to offer arguments about its phony concerns for women, saying that abortion causes breast cancer and mental illness (repeatedly disproved by actual research), and that it wants to stop legal abortion for women's own good. This argument requires a lot of ignoring of the fact that back-alley abortions tend to be not so great for women, but Team Fetus is trying its best.

Unfortunately, the mainstream media buys right into the "pro-life" front, portraying the battle over abortion as an intractable one of Team Fetus versus The Feminists, fighting over life versus women's rights, which does indeed sound like a horribly complex struggle in which neither side gets to claim moral superiority.

It's also complete bullshit. The real battle is between sexual liberationists and misogynist conservatives who see abortion as the most important front in their war against sex. Call them the Anti-Sex League or the Victorian Wannabes, but just don't call them "pro-life," especially since most are proud conservatives who back up imperialist wars and stalwartly oppose things that would actually preserve life, like universal health care. I call them anti-choice.

Anti-choicers may be crazy, but they're not stupid. They get that just coming straight out against sex wouldn't win them many friends, since sex continues its millennia-unbroken record of wild popularity. And, to be fair, they don't disapprove of every single instance in which a penis enters a vagina. (Every time a penis enters an anus is a different story, especially if the anus also belongs to a man.) If the penis is wielded by a man who is married to the woman sporting the vagina, and there is a mild to strong risk that this act will result in a baby, the anti-choice movement can accept that. But everything else needs to be punished. Straight couples who have sex outside of marriage are particularly interesting to anti-choicers, who would like to see more accidental pregnancies that result in shotgun weddings.

How can we know this? Well, despite the mainstream media's continuing inability to get it, we have tons of evidence. Anti-abortion activists can be counted on to resist anything they see as interfering with their goals of getting everyone into either a married-virgins or a shotgun wedding that leads to a boring, sexless marriage marked by resentment that's alleviated only by going to your local evangelical church to fight against a younger generation's finding the happiness that eludes you.

Who do you think is behind the abstinence-only education in schools that teaches your kids that condoms don't work (by implying that you shouldn't even bother with them if you do have sex)? Who do you think lobbied the Bush administration into defunding UNFPA, an international organization that provides contraception but not abortion? Who threw a giant fit when a vaccine to prevent HPV, and therefore cervical cancer, came out, because it meant the anti-choicers couldn't scare fornicating teenagers with cervical cancer anymore? Who got the FDA to stall the release of over-the-counter emergency contraception because they feared it would lead to teenage sex cults (actual quote from a Bush-era FDA employee)? Who successfully pressures many Republican congressmen to vote against Title X family-planning funding that makes contraception affordable to lower-income Americans and teenagers? Hell, who do you think tries to restrict gay rights and "cure" people of homosexuality?

If you guessed that Team Fetus and the anti-sex crazies are one and the same, you'd be right. They persist even though many of the other things they resist—emergency contraception, affordable condoms, and gay sex—keep women from getting pregnant by accident, and if women aren't getting pregnant by accident, they aren't getting abortions. (I mean, you could *try,* but most doctors won't perform an abortion if there's no pregnancy to abort.) You'd think that people who don't want fetuses dying needlessly would be interested in ways to stop that from happening, such as increasing the use of contraception. But Team Fetus goes out of its way to make sure that the number-one cause of abortion—unintended pregnancy—will go up, not down. Very peculiar, unless you accept that they're a bunch of filthy liars who are more interested in controlling and punishing sexuality, especially female sexuality, and that fetal life is, at best, a secondary concern of theirs.

But just because the anti-choice movement is composed of a bunch of filthy liars doesn't mean that people like it when you state so bluntly, I've discovered. Out in the blogging world, I often write about the filthy-liar aspects of the anti-choice movement, and I almost always get some comment or email that is a variation of "Hey! Someone I know isn't really against sex or birth control, but they still think killing a fetus is wrong. How about the person I know?"

This is a version of the eternal evil/stupid problem when it comes to conservatives. Do they believe harmful things (such as that abortion should be illegal, which harms women on many levels) because they're too evil to care or because they're too stupid to know better? The stereotypical good-hearted pro-lifer who really cares about fetuses and never even thinks about the sex that created fetuses would be an example of the far end of the evil/stupid continuum. Do these people exist? Probably, though I've found that most who show up to make this claim will fall apart and start screeching about how sluts need to keep their legs closed if they don't want to have babies, if you apply enough pressure. But I'd like to give the benefit of the doubt to the people claiming they know someone who might be on the purely stupid side of the scale. It's certainly possible.

Do these genuine fetus lovers who have no problem with female sexuality exist in sufficient numbers to make any difference whatsoever? No, of course not. You can predict people's attitudes about other feminist issues pretty accurately if they announce up front that they're "pro-life"—and those attitudes won't be good. But media types and politicians continue to pursue the mythical, nonmisogynist pro-lifer as if this person has the key to ending the most played-out, inflexible debate in our society. Especially after Obama took office, there was a lot of talk about finding common ground between pro-choicers and anti-abortion activists, based on the naive assumption that you could get everyone on board with at least agreeing to reduce the need for abortion. Sure, pro-choicers can be counted on to sign up for anything that helps women avoid the need for outpatient surgery, but that's always been true.

So far, this has turned out to be an epic failure, because you can't really find common ground when one side is fronting about its true intentions. Pro-lifers routinely reject any solutions that allow women to escape punishment for fucking, such as better access to contraception and better sex education. Since those are pretty much the only ways to reduce the abortion rate, the common ground between the crazies and the noncrazies falls apart in the first step of negotiations. So far, the Democrats have crafted a number of bills aimed at reducing the abortion rate by increasing access to contraception and by providing a better safety net for mothers, and those bills usually fail because all the fetus worshippers who swear that abortion is the greatest human-rights crisis since the Holocaust refuse to sign on, because they don't generally approve of social spending and they're holding out for a bill that bans sluttiness.

So while I completely understand the urge to assume the best about your political opponents, and to take their words at face value instead of just dismissing them as filthy fucking liars, as a public service, I must recommend that you give up hoping for the kindhearted anti-abortion activist to appear. So much time has already been wasted writing bills the anti-choicers won't vote for, starting discussions they won't join, and giving them the benefit of the doubt while they run around starting crisis pregnancy centers to tell women that birth control will poison them. Time that could have been spent listening to music, working on hobbies, or having delicious, decadent sex.

BIRTH CONTROL PILLS
for a Cleaner Planet and a Better Economy

It's one of the most prescribed drugs in the country. People know it on sight from its blister pack, whether it's rectangular or circular. It's been around since it effectively ended the post–World War II baby boom. Women take it for years, often decades. It's so well known and ubiquitous that people simply call it "the Pill." If pills were rock bands, the Pill would be the Beatles.

Despite its pedigree, the Pill still makes people think mostly of sex. In a sense, this is fair: You take it so you can have sex without getting pregnant. Stating it baldly like this tends to make people squirm, though. Perhaps if pills were bands, the Pill—well, at least its reputation—would be the Velvet Underground, grasped immediately by the few, slowly spreading as people grow accustomed to the idea, but still mostly underground. Even now that we're into the twenty-first century, I find that a shocking number of women I meet who are on the Pill treat having sex without getting pregnant as merely a pleasant side effect that had no bearing on their choice to start taking the Pill. "Some people *need* it," they'll say defensively. "I have menstrual cramps and the worst mood swings." Not to bag on their reasons, of course, but it does make me wonder: If there were a pill out there that granted you a super-power, like telekinesis, and simultaneously got rid of your acne, would people insist that they were just in it to clear up their skin, and that their ability to move objects with their minds was just a lucky accident?

Sex makes people stupid, at least when women have it. Even very pro-gressive people who grasp intellectually that there's nothing wrong with ladies fucking—and that being able to do so without getting pregnant is a laudable superpower—still get squirmy when it's shoved right in their face. The plain little Pill pack dredges up all sorts of thoughts and concerns about sex, all our obsessive worrying about whether it's the right guy, the right time, done after the right amount of hand-wringing—are we 100 percent sure this is empowering? Even if there's a stripper pole? These are all fun questions, but they tend to crowd out the fact that the Pill is about a lot more than whether or not doggy-style sex is feminist (or whether or not the trust levels in the relationship affect that).

We think the Pill is about sex, but it's more accurate to say it's about babies. Or, to be even more clear, it's about not having babies—whether that means not now, not ever, or not after a given number. Babies are a less sexy topic than sex is, but they're probably more important at the end of the day, if only because your screaming kid will probably wake up the neighbors more surely than your screaming orgasms ever could.

It's not a coincidence that the anti-choice movement, while treating abortion as public enemy number one, considers the birth control pill number two. The American Life League even stages an annual protest against the decision that legalized the Pill, *Griswold v. Connecticut.* Technically, it legal-ized all forms of contraception for married people, but the anti-choicers focus most of their hate on the Pill, by calling the day Pill Kills Day. There's some elaborate, bullshit excuse for why the Pill is somehow worse than the condom (or the anti-choice movement's only allowable method, the nonworking, er, rhythm method), but it's obvious to anyone with a proper lack of naiveté that the Pill offends because the Pill *works*. Hormonal birth control ranks only below sterilization in effectiveness. That's a whole lot of sluts getting away with something, in the eyes of anti-choice nutters, and for the rest of us, that's a whole lot of opportunity for most people to have as many children as they want, but no more.

And it turns out that, given a choice, people don't actually want that many kids. Throughout the 1950s, the annual birthrate held at about twenty-five births per thousand people. It started to sink after that, but following *Griswold*, it slipped into the teens. Now it's about fourteen births per thousand people. People didn't stop liking babies, but, as with most pleasures, a little moderation goes a long way, and baby love is no exception. And, hell, now baby teetotalers are growing in number and becoming downright unremarkable.

But if you look beyond just the individual benefit of minimizing the number of shitting, crying babies you have to deal with in your lifetime, the completely voluntary population-control situation we've got now has also been a boon to the big picture. The environment immediately comes to mind. Global warming has already gotten out of control, and we may not be able to reverse its effects, so we could all be doomed. That said, we would have been doomed a hell of a lot sooner if we had 56 percent more babies each year. That's a 56 percent greater need to buy minivans to belch carbon emissions into the air, 56 percent more fresh customers for McDonald's hamburgers, with all the attendant damage done that meat production does to our atmosphere, and 56 percent more customers every year, period, with each step of manufacturing and transportation spilling more emissions into our environment. Since Americans contribute more carbon to the atmosphere per capita than any other group of people on the planet, no one is weeping that we at least found one way to cut back. We weren't willing to give up our SUVs and our heavy meat consumption, so we're bad on the "per," but we cut back on babies, so we spared the world a few more years on the basis of the "capita."

Talking about overpopulation on the left raises hackles. I could feel the room stiffen during a showing of *An Inconvenient Truth* when Al Gore demonstrated that skyrocketing populations correlated to skyrocketing global warming. And it's not without good reason. "Overpopulation" was a rallying cry for decades for racists who were totally willing to exploit genuine concerns to imply that only certain colors of people needed to cut back on the baby habit, by force if necessary. During the 1960s and '70s, the main concerns about global overpopulation centered on food production and on whether supply could keep up with demand, but innovations in agriculture made that issue moot, leaving only the racists to think that there were too many people of this type of ethnicity or that if they saw them in public at all. So I cannot ever blame people who just get upset about the discussion and won't even talk about it. They have a reason.

But times have changed, and the racist right, while not giving up on its strategy of trying to stop women of color from having babies, has shifted most of its focus to forcing all women into childbirth, in the hope that white women will step up production. Meanwhile, global warming has become an emergency situation, and even the methods of agriculture that we developed to keep up with the exploding population feed global warming. The good news is that most people don't want to have a shit-ton of kids. From a liberal perspective, you couldn't ask for a better problem to tackle, because the solution not only doesn't require even the slightest coercion, it actually comes from a place of increasing freedom.

People like fucking and they don't like having kids all the time. Birth control sells itself. In fact, 98 percent of women will use it at some point in their lives, even with the religious right telling them that contraception melts their eyeballs while turning them into dirty whores. Even marijuana can't claim that kind of success rate. And let's face it—people are a lot more likely to whip out a joint and smoke it in front of you than they are to let you see their birth control pills, even by accident. That birth control wins out over that level of shame and fear tells you something about its popularity. I've spent a lot of time in this book talking about how going green is more fun than you'd think, but worry-free fucking probably does beat even tankless water heaters in the game of having fun while doing your part for the planet.

The economic arguments for a voluntary population-reduction program of unfettered fucking are a little harder to promote than the straightforward environmental claim that less people equals less pollution. But even from the most staid economic viewpoint, which favors the rich over the rest of us and relies on figures like the GDP to measure the entire economy, there's a valid case for fewer babies. As Michelle Goldberg notes in her book *The Means of Reproduction,* there's reason to believe that the Japanese economy bounced back after World War II because people began severely limiting their families (mostly through abortion, which is much more accepted in Japan), and the smaller the percentage of a population that's dependent, the more productive it is. It's hard to deny that in the United States, women can work because they don't have to spend as much time chasing kids around, and that makes us more productive.

But if that's so, then why on earth does the Republican party coddle the forced birth brigade, when it seems to be against corporate America's best interests to move such a huge percentage of the population from the "working for the weekends" category to the "can't work, too busy changing diapers" category? Mostly, I think it has to do with consumer culture and the need for perpetual growth in profit margins. More babies doesn't look like fewer workers to corporate America. They look like more minivans and Tickle Me Elmos moving off the lot. Corporate America doesn't tend to ask hard questions about where the money to buy these things will come from, and if you doubt this, reconsider how our entire economy went under in no small part because big banks didn't ask if huge numbers of people would be able to afford mortgages.

Less controversial is how birth control helps people on the microeconomics level, or what politicians like to call Main Street, which they contrast with the decrepitude of Wall Street, the institution that actually holds their attention when they're not campaigning. From our capitalist masters' point of view, it doesn't matter how many people you have in your house as long as you spend money, but for people actually trying to manage household finances, the math is easy: Women's ability in the past few decades to limit their births and hit the job market has kept many middle-class households safely in the middle-class territory. If any belief defines liberals, it's wanting a large, healthy middle class, and birth control made that possible, even in eras when union busting became acceptable again and many new jobs created involved asking if you want fries with that.

And if a low birthrate endangers our consumption-centered economy, so what? The hip new word now is "sustainability," and even though it's hip, that doesn't mean it's meaningless. It means moving toward an economy where we manage to get by without sucking the planet and the people dry in an ever-elusive quest for economic growth. Sustainability is about creating an economy where people don't have to work harder every year or the planet doesn't have to give up more resources than it has to keep our economy functioning. Unfortunately, it's treated like a buzzword, and it looks like sustainability is going to become a reality only if the issue is forced.

That can happen in two ways: Either the planet can give out, or the growth rate of consumption will give out first. If you enjoy living on the planet, then you should root for the latter. There have been some minor, hippie-ish attempts to force the issue by reducing, reusing, and recycling, and efforts like Buy Nothing Day. These are doomed to fail because of lack of interest. But falling birth rates present a lot of promise. Corporate America can find ways to maximize the consumption per capita, so if we reduce the capita, we won't help it achieve its goal of maintaining an economy built on growth at all costs. In other words, we're probably not going to get people to beat corporate America on the "per"—we all find ourselves drawn to the sixty-four-ounce drink over the forty-four-ounce one—but we can eagerly beat it on the "capita."

The best part is that muscling the powers that be into finding more sustainable economic strategies can be accomplished most effectively through methods that don't require self-deprivation. Enjoy yourselves! Take some time off and fuck to your heart's content. Lie in bed eating bonbons between bouts of copulation. Watch some porn and spray some more semen all over the place. Just do it while using contraception, and you'll be doing your part to stick it to the Man. It's like punk rock, but for everyone who likes fucking.

GIVING,
TALKING, AND
Outing Pro-Lifers

— 66 ! 99 —

In general, I try to avoid reducing people to their wallets, reasoning that most of us aren't rich, and really, it seems likes it's on the rich first to start giving all their money away before the rest of us feel like we have to. That said, when it comes to reproductive justice, I have to point out that money you give is often money that you can be assured goes straight to a visible, good cause, particularly if you give to Planned Parenthood or another group that both offers medical care and fights for a good cause. If you give to an abortion fund, it goes straight to someone who needs to pay for an abortion. Doesn't really get more transparent than that, and unlike with campaign donations, you don't feel like you're gambling.

The pro-choice movement really faces an unfairly lopsided

situation when it comes to financing. Our opposition doesn't offer services, just propaganda, and so it can make its money go a whole lot further in marketing appeals than pro-choicers could even dream of. That's why there are many times more crisis pregnancy centers that try to bully scared pregnant women out of getting abortions than there are actual family-planning clinics that offer abortion services. It's cheaper to give someone a $2 pregnancy test, tell her abortion kills babies, and hand her a diaper and a teddy bear extracted from an arcade game than it is to provide actual, expensive medical care. Since we can't morally justify ceasing services and dedicating all pro-choice donations into marketing, this is just the way things are. But it's all the more reason to put a family-planning clinic or abortion fund at the top of your charity list when it comes time to start spreading what little money you have around.

Okay, begging over. (Phew.) Now, here's the fun part about what you can do to further the cause of reproductive rights: Open your mouth and talk. Or flip open your laptop and write. Big mouths can make big changes, and while the anti-choice movement makes like it was a bunch of somber intellectuals in judges' robes who got abortion legalized, those judges did it only after being subjected to the arguments and opinions of women who never learned that good girls are to be seen and not heard.

If you've ever had an abortion, consider talking about it in a public forum. Not many women do, so it's surprisingly easy to get published talking about abortion. Or, if that scares you, write it on a blog. Abortion is the most common outpatient procedure in the country: Twice as many are performed every year as are open-heart surgeries or hysterectomies, but you'd never know it. A whole lot of people think they don't know anyone who's had an abortion. They're wrong. But they're not going to know that—know that women who've had abortions aren't actually baby-killing witches who get pregnant so they can sacrifice their fetuses to Baal—unless more women start putting a human face on the procedure.

From my long and at times surreal experience in the trenches of talking smack to anti-choicers and educating people about the reality of the debate, I've found that one of the most important things you can talk about is the anti-choice movement's hostility to contraception. This tends to get people out of the rut of talking about how "both sides" have a point, and both sides are crazy, and both sides blah blah blah. This simple fact—that every single anti-choice group in the country is hostile to contraception, and many advocate openly for banning it—disrupts the entire narrative. Makes people realize that the mainstream media's image of anti-choicers as hyper-religious but largely harmless fetus lovers who are, at worst, a little unrealistic is complete bullshit. They're more than a little unrealistic. They think they can actually bring the long-popular practice of sexual intercourse to a halt. (Or most of it—in the dark, missionary sex between married couples with an intent to procreate will always be accepted as a necessary evil.) Most people grasp that contraception prevents abortion, and so the only reason the Fetus

"!"
GETTING PAST
Will & Grace:
GLBTQ RIGHTS

CHAPTER SEVEN

FUNDIES GOT ONE THING RIGHT:
Gay Marriage Threatens "Traditional" Marriage

The march toward nationwide equal marriage rights for same-sex marriage has turned into a jog, and as I write this, the victories are piling up so fast that I fear referencing any of them, lest doing so dates this book immediately. For all I know, by the time this book hits the shelves of your local library or bookstore, the Supreme Court will have had a chance to weigh in, and the odds seem very high that the same court that overturned sodomy laws in 2003 will find that same-sex couples have the same right that straight people currently enjoy to torture their friends and relatives with registries, destination weddings, bachelor/bachelorette parties, inheritance rights, and joint health insurance—facts that will probably seem like yesterday's news as the wedding industrial complex swarms in to take full financial advantage of the situation.

How do homophobes react to the situation? By declaring same-sex marriage a threat to traditional marriage. In fact, at this point, you'd be hard-pressed to get fundies to say that they oppose same-sex marriage. Oh, no—they just *support* traditional marriage, which will collapse the day two dudes in tuxes get married with Uncle Sam's blessing. Most organizations that oppose gay rights do so under names that imply they're protecting people instead of hurting people, such as the anti-gay organizations National Organization for Marriage and California's Protect Marriage.

This argument confuses supporters of gay rights. How, we reasonably ask, can a couple of married dudes down the street really impact your marriage? If you get divorced because ladies can marry ladies and dudes can marry dudes, then your marriage was on its last legs anyway, and you were just looking for an excuse to get out of it.

Clearly, the gay-marriage opponents are lying about protecting straight married people, which is pretty standard wingnut procedure, right? After all, we're talking about the same activists who will tell you to your face, without even blinking, that abortion causes breast cancer. Their other reasons to oppose gay marriage—that it represents religious persecution of conservatives, that they give a shit about the children—are pretty obviously invalid, so this traditional-marriage platform must be, too, right?

Yes and no. Often, you'll hear some no-brained motherfucker claim he's supporting traditional marriage, when he obviously doesn't even know what he's talking about, since he's just coughing up right-wing talking points. He's the guy who will tell you he opposes Obama because he's a "socialist," but when he's asked to define "socialist," he'll stammer and try to escape.

That said, there's a sliver of truth to the claims that same-sex marriage poses a threat to traditional marriage, which is why this argument sticks a little better than the more obvious bullshit conservatives spew. The fundies are right: Same-sex marriage *does* present a threat to traditional marriage, depending on your definition of "traditional."

For fundies, "traditional" means a whole lot more than merely pairing a man with a woman and calling it a day. "Traditional marriage" implies a power imbalance: The husband is the head of the household, and the woman provides sex, housework, heirs, and childcare in exchange for not getting called a spinster. (As an aside, many feminist-minded women throughout history saw how unfair this exchange was and muscled through the s-word to become, among other things, Jane Austen.) Same-sex couples present a very confusing challenge to this notion. To quote many homophobes I've had the displeasure of hearing making unfunny jokes about gay couples they encounter, "Who's the husband?" Which means, how do they decide who has to wash the dishes while his significant other watches TV? How do they decide who has to do all the sexual servicing and who gets to come every time without even pausing to wonder what's wrong with this situation? Who has to keep track of birthdays, anniversaries, parties, and other social-calendar stuff, and who gets to use that part of his brain to memorize sports statistics? In the narcissistic wingnut's mind, the confusion these questions cause is enough to demand that others sacrifice their basic human rights.

Gay-rights supporters' natural response to this demand is to point out that existing laws do not necessarily determine who gets to control the remote. There's legal equality in heterosexual marriages, and all those evil old laws (well, most of them) that make women servile to men are gone. Women can sue for divorce, own property, say no to sex, and even keep their own names. The law can't stop a straight married couple from dividing chores equally, making decisions through consensus instead of penile fiat, and even name the kids after the one who pushed them painfully out of her body. If you want to protect traditional marriage, we could argue, it's too late—the horse done left the barn.

If fundies weren't so busy trying to seem like they're on the side of purity, angels, and goodness itself, they'd probably have a right to laugh at us for this argument. The theoretical egalitarian straight marriage hasn't done much to provide for the realistically egalitarian straight marriage. Yes, heterosexual coupling is far less oppressive than ever before, but let's face it: Most dishes in these houses are washed by female hands. Ninety percent of American wives capitulate to social demands and male egos and rename themselves after their husbands, and even more name the children after their husbands, as if he were the one who birthed them. Wishing for egalitarian marriages hasn't done much to make them happen. We need a more dramatic shift in our understanding of what marriage *is* before we can get past traditional marriage.

Right-wingers clearly think that same-sex marriage will provide this shift and will redefine marriage not as a way to formalize male dominance over women, one couple at a time, but as a partnership. It's hard to see why they're so panicked, though. Having a married lesbian couple down the street might push straight couples out of the inertia that forces her to take on more responsibility while he gets most decision-making power. But then again, most marriages I'm familiar with are striving to be egalitarian and failing. Maybe in wingnut marriages, mere exposure to same-sex couples will cause wives to rebel and say, "Heeeeeeeyyyyyyyyyy, Ann does the dishes and Diana washes the floors. How come I have to do both?"

Or maybe this isn't about household chores at all, but about sex. Isn't it always? Right-wing fear of women's independence always has a strong element of fear of male impotence behind it: *If women learn something about the world, they'll start wanting satisfaction in bed, and what if I can't perform? Then I'm not a real man!* After decades of painting homosexuals as sexual libertines who'll stop at nothing for sexual satisfaction, right-wingers must find it downright scary to imagine said libertines entering the sacred chamber of marital boredom. Married known libertines could signal to the world at large that it's not impossible to be married and have hot sex. The excuses for being a bad lover are quickly running out for the lazy husbands of the world.

THE HOMOSEXUAL AGENDA
Is Playing at My House

In many respects, the much reviled and much reported (in conservative media) Homosexual Agenda has been a resounding success. Granted, we've failed at the goals that conservatives outlined for the agenda—so far, no pristine straight children of right-wing Republicans have been turned into homosexuals, though some did come out of the closet due to a previously held sexual orientation—but outside of that, the Homosexual Agenda has kicked a remarkable amount of ass in a short period of time.

Gay marriage in the '90s was such a never-gonna-happen fantasy that politicians thought god had given it to them as a barnstorming political distraction. No one seriously thought at the time that we'd see legal gay marriage anytime soon, but that didn't stop politicians (including Bill Clinton) from looking for every opportunity to ban this practice that wasn't legal to begin with. States banned it and banned it again. Congress, with Bill Clinton's eager cooperation, passed the Defense of Marriage Act to keep nonexistent legal gay marriages from moving from their fantasy states to real states and spreading the contagion of gay couples who mind their own business and go about their day like every other married couple.

And let's not even talk about "Don't Ask, Don't Tell," the Clinton-esque noncompromise wherein gay people get to stay in the military as long as they are simply not gay in the vicinity of anyone with the powers of perception and loose lips. That this was considered some remarkable show of tolerance in the '90s shows exactly how far we've come.

The glorious Homosexual Agenda has done a bang-up job in the subsequent years. It got gay marriage legalized in Iowa, for instance, and there's not much you can add to that, except to repeat it: It got gay marriage legalized in Iowa. And other states. And the sky didn't fall in. Hate-crimes legislations and civil-rights protections are rapidly spreading, and conservatives have all but given up pretending that people who don't want to get gay-bashed or fired are asking for "special rights."

But really, where the progress is most shocking is in the hearts-and-minds department. Just looking at polling trends will make the most numerically daft person say, "No shit?" In 1995, only six states saw approval for gay marriage above 30 percent—all those states now top 50 percent. Gay marriage used to be a never-gonna-happen issue, but recent polling data shows that a plurality of people support gay marriage, and only 28 percent disapprove of either gay marriage or civil unions. In 2000, California banned gay marriage with 61 percent of the vote, and when it came up on the ballot again in 2008, the ban barely passed, with 52 percent of the vote, after anti-gay forces spent the most money on the ballot initiative in the history of ballot initiatives. Most observers think that when gay marriage comes up for a vote again in California, it will win, as the people who voted against it this time are becoming ashamed of being such giant assholes.

Progress has been made on levels that are hard to measure, as the Homosexual Agenda—while still unable to recruit the wholesome straight kids of fundamentalists with promises of white weddings where the

Homosexual Agenda spins records at the reception—has created this situation where straight people personally know gay people. And I don't mean they suspect it or have heard rumors about it. I mean your coworker/friend/relative brought his or her same-sex partner to happy hour, and it turned out that it wasn't a big deal at all. It's not showing my age to say I remember when that *wasn't* true at all, because I'm not that old—it just happened that fast. A decade ago, most of the time people you met didn't come out to you unless they'd really gotten to know you and trust you, and even then, much of the time it was obviously nerve-racking. Now, you hear even straight people refer to the same-sex couples in their lives with the words "boy/girlfriend" or "husband/wife" without pausing to make sure you heard them correctly, so you can either be scandalized (if the speaker is conservative) or be aware of how *tolerant* the straight person is (if the person is liberal). It just is.

Indeed, the Homosexual Agenda has been so roundly successful that famous actors and musicians who are gay can be profiled in major magazines and newspapers that find their sexual orientation so unremarkable it can go without mention. Not because they're hiding it, but because going out of your way to mention something that's not scandalous seems beside the point nowadays.

Too bad no one alerted the Democrats in D.C. to this trend. Apparently, once you step on the Hill, all understanding that most Americans believe gays deserve equal rights seeps out of your brain. It's like stepping into a time machine that transports you to an era when the only people who aren't scandalized by homosexuality are gays themselves and a few straight bohemians who don't have any money, anyway. This, despite the presence of openly gay politicians in Congress.

How else do you explain why politicians like Barack Obama—who was all about equality on the campaign trail, and making promises to kill

"Don't Ask, Don't Tell" and honor civil unions (even if he wouldn't use the word "marriage")—suddenly get cold feet in office and dawdle on these issues, or, worse, why the Department of Justice files briefs that suggest that legal gay marriage opens the door to child abuse? How do you explain the skittishness of Democratic Congress critters in general, even though all the polling data they could hope to hang on to shows that their voters really don't have a problem with gay marriage? The gap between Americans' liberalizing attitudes on gay rights and Democrats in Congress continues to grow at an exponential rate, and no one can quite figure out why. Perhaps congressional Republicans are feeding Democrats hallucinogens that make them believe it's 1994 all over again.

Or maybe it's misplaced pity for their Republican colleagues that makes Democrats forget basic sense. After all, while it's true that support for gay rights keeps growing dramatically, the hardcore-conservative base will be easy to sway for years into coming out to vote for Republicans just by being told that the Homosexual Agenda is coming to recruit their kids. If gays really do get equal rights, that takes the punch out of that fear, and without that issue to raise hell about, many Republicans will be floating around lost, hoping to get people all riled up because there's sex on TV but failing miserably.

If misplaced pity is in fact the cause of their reluctance, then D.C. Democrats had better wake up. More of us are joining the Homosexual Agenda every day now, and if they don't play a little catch-up, they'll get lapped.

EVEN IF THEY FIND THE CAUSE, Do We Want a Cure?

As far as public-opinion shifts go, gay-rights activists should throw themselves a parade (on top of gay-pride parades) celebrating their truly remarkable success. As I documented in the last chapter, things that seemed nearly unthinkable a decade ago, such as gay marriage, now have an air of inevitability about them. Gay marriage, partner benefits, laws against housing and employment discrimination—soon the entire checklist of gay-rights items will be filled and everyone can pack up and go home, right?

Well, of course you know I'm going to say no. One of the benefits and drawbacks of being a good liberal is that you get to emulate some of the more popular superheroes and declare that your work is never done. It's beneficial because it alleviates boredom, but it's disturbing because it means you can never kick back and have a beer, satisfied that your work is done. Of course, that means that instead you should just kick back and have a beer on a regular basis, because your work is never done, so maybe we should put the "endless stream of shit to do" strongly in the plus category. You can sleep when you're dead.

The gay-rights movement should study the reproductive-rights movement closely to absorb the dangers of resting on your laurels after a major victory. In the 1950s through the '70s, feminists and sexual-health advocates managed to help get the birth control pill invented, legalize contraception, legalize abortion, institute sex education, and decouple the right to birth control and education from the institution of marriage. That sort of string of victories would give anyone reason to think that the forces of good have won out. Most Americans agreed with the intellectual arguments for abortion rights and rightfully thought of the wackaloons who protest abortion clinics as relics of an older social order of injustice and hostile anti-sex attitudes. Most Americans have sex out of wedlock and enjoy the benefits of contraception, and by "most," I mean 95 percent and 98 percent, respectively. You'd be Sarah Palin levels of stupid not to read that as a resounding victory on its surface.

Except. Except that the work of convincing Americans that women who have sex really, truly aren't bad people was never completely finished. A quick perusal of the tabloid section at the supermarket should confirm this fact. Hell, the popularity of up-skirt shots of a variety of starlets should indicate that, not only is there an enormous audience for the message "Women who have sex should be *ashamed*," but there's also an enormous audience for the message "Women who have pussies are so disgusting that it should be national news." (I do enjoy imagining the intended audience picking up a magazine and saying, "Lindsay Lohan has a vulva? Does her mother know about this?") Now, Americans think of women fucking in roughly the same light in which they think of marijuana—everyone does it, no one really minds it, but there's a consensus that we should maintain an official disapproval for no real reason whatsoever. And if innocent people get hurt, that's just the price you pay.

The tolerant view Americans have of hypocrisy is the only reason the anti-choice movement has a foothold. Usually, we don't let raving maniacs who hate half the population and want to see them relegated to lives of debased servility get on TV to pretend they're normal people with reasonable opinions. But we make an exception for the anti-choice nuts, because they're able to exploit people's lingering prejudices against women who have sex. Abstinence-only rode into public schools by exploiting that same ambiguity. Most people expect that kids will have sex for fun, and not strictly to procreate, at some point in their lives, and that they have a right to have and know how to use contraception for that occasion. But we allowed a handful of lunatics who sincerely thought they could push their "do it only for the babies" message to control the schools for a time, mostly because most Americans never completely embraced the most fundamental beliefs of sexual liberation and feminism. Logic and reason will take you only so far. People have to believe what you're saying on a gut level, so that preferably they're spouting it when they've had one too many.

The lesson regarding gay rights is this: We can't quit just because a majority of Americans already believe gays deserve equal rights and because this belief is reflected in laws. People will always be open to homophobic arguments as long as they think of homosexuality as remarkable. In other words, the marker for success should be an end to the question of what "causes" homosexuality.

I'm fine with questions about what causes sexual orientation in general. If science demonstrates that certain hormone levels or genes or other factors push some people toward gay and others toward straight, then that's interesting but largely apolitical information. The problem is when you start to think of one category as the default and the other as a deviation. Right now, most people think of homosexuality the same way Freud thought of women:

He thought they were like men without penises, and that that idea explained what was wrong or broken about them. In theory, he could have just as easily thought men were women who didn't get a period, but obviously, his sexism instead caused him to think women actually cast around listlessly, despairing that we can merely create life instead of do neat things like try to hit a target with a urine stream.

Right now, most discussions about the source of sexual orientation are about the cause of homosexuality, as if you could change the cause and the individual would revert to the default of heterosexuality. Naturally, wingnuts spend the most amount of energy worrying about this question, writing screeds like the one in which James Dobson suggested that fathers can prevent their sons (it's always the boys they worry about) from turning gay by showering with them at a young age, so they can get a full eyeball of daddy dick. (I'm still not entirely sure why Dobson thought this would work.) Of course, the very same people try to play off homosexuality as a choice, more like an addiction than like a sexual orientation. Most Americans don't see it as a choice and are coming around to the idea that you're a full person if you're gay, but they're reserving a belief that homosexuality is a deviation that happens when otherwise straight people are changed by an errant gene or an early childhood experience.

What we need is for people to think of sexual orientation the same way they've come around to thinking of handedness. Most people are right-handed, but some people are left-handed, and this fact tends to be considered wholly unremarkable and unnecessary to explain. Not that it was always that way, since many people remember the hellish era, not too long ago, when lefties were tortured with mandatory right-handed scissor use or even spankings for using the wrong hand. But this just means we can take heart. Things that once wrongly seemed like perverse deviations, like left-handedness, can transfer into the largely unremarkable evidence-of-diversity column within a generation.

Or at least they can if we stay on it. Which means that even after we secure marriage and laws against hate crimes and bans on anti-gay discrimination, we need to get people to start seeing what's wrong with the question when you ask what "causes" homosexuality. As a side goal, we should also encourage straight people to stop looking at gay couples and asking which one's the husband.

COME OUT,
REGARDLESS OF
Your Orientation

Being a straight woman who has lived with all the attendant privileges for most of my life, I'm not going to insult anyone's intelligence by going over the same old ground that gay-rights activists have perfected in appeals to gay people to step out of the closet and live their lives publicly, making the rest of boneheaded straight society realize that "gay" isn't actually scary, much less the End of Life as We Know It.

So instead I'll talk about what straight allies can do that we're not doing enough of. (And you know it, straight readers!) We're not coming out. We're hiding behind our straight privilege when we hear other straight people say homophobic things. We have the luxury of pretending we didn't hear that and going along, because it's not about us. And we know what will happen if we do confront homophobes—they'll get in our faces, demanding to know why we're such politically correct bores, and maybe even trying to play it off like they're not really homophobic (nudge, nudge). No one enjoys that confrontation, so it's often easier to just let it go than it is to speak up.

Well, quit it. We suck as allies if we can't do our gay friends and neighbors this simple courtesy. Why do they have to do all the work? We can take our lumps, and frankly, we owe them that much.

I think you'll find that once you start coming out as an ally of gay people when you come across straight people who say homophobic things, it gets easier with time. What begins as a quietly mumbled "Excuse me, but I have gay friends and they're very nice and I don't like it when you say things like that about them and you don't know them anyway and can't you just be nicer about it?" will, with time and experience in confronting homophobes, turn into "Take your goddamn gay jokes on a long walk off a short pier, asswipe. And go fuck yourself while you're at it, because god knows no one else should do it." I suppose some mealymouthed types would say that approach is ineffectual, but I find it actually causes people to be a lot more careful about what kinds of stupid shit they'll say. Plus, how many opportunities do you have to relieve some stress by cussing out some dipshit? It's surprisingly relaxing, once you work up the courage to do it.

"!"
DON'T FEAR
LEAVING
Your House:
The War on Terror

CHAPTER EIGHT

TERRORISTS:
The New Communists

Within moments of President Obama's first actions to move away from the Bush administration's policy of torturing at random and holding detainees indefinitely without charge, the screaming began, most of it referencing fictional character Jack Bauer from the show *24*. On January 23, 2009, the notoriously wingnutty *Wall Street Journal* editorial page, while using scare quotes around the word "torture" to describe techniques that the entire civilized world (excepting American wingnuts) believes to be torture, hysterically suggested that Obama would punish American heroes whose willingness to use a liberal dose of undeniable torture saved cities from terrorist nuclear attacks.

> *No one may be willing to be Jack Bauer when Mr. Obama really needs him. This will have consequences for U.S. safety, and for the Obama Administration if there is another 9/11.*

In the minds of the wingnutteria, 24 is a documentary and we didn't stop 9/11 because we didn't torture enough cab drivers picked up for walking around the wrong neighborhood. In reality, we didn't even pick up anyone with a connection to 9/11 beforehand because of failures in the nontorturing departments, and terrorists fall into Jack Bauer's torturing hands because the writers can make them. I haven't watched the show, so I can't say how the wingnuts explain away what seems the largest flaw in the torture-confession-prevention cycle, which is that the torturing victim invested in making a terrorist plot go forward merely has to lie.

This is how I imagine an average episode of *24* goes:

> *Jack Bauer: Where's the bomb?!*
>
> *Terrorist scum: (Spits on floor.) Infidel! Do you think I'd tell a dog like you? After all, we are trying to kill millions of people because we hate freedom, and we won't stop until Bush admits that his wife is sexually unsatisfied. I also have some more baffling reasons for my behavior that have nothing to do with Western imperialism, if you'd like to hear them.*
>
> *Jack: What if I apply some electrodes to a TV-safe word for "cock"?*
>
> *Terrorist scum: Okay! I'll tell you. There's a nuke in a school, a hospital, and a generic-looking church that could be yours, the viewer at home.*

I can also imagine a more realistic, if less dramatic, way this might go, if a real-life Jack Bauer managed to hit the one in a gazillion chance of getting to a terrorist who is about to set off a nuclear bomb, when he knows for a fact that the terrorist knows the information, but he doesn't know what the information is. I imagine that Bauer would ride to this interrogation on a unicorn.

> Jack: (Unicorn rears up dramatically, shaking his horn, threatening the terrorist scum.) Where's the bomb?!

> Terrorist scum: Nice horse.

> Jack: Tell me or I'll waterboard you!

> Terrorist scum: It's in your wife's bedroom, where she's conveniently having sex with the lover you know nothing of.

> (Jack rides off to his house to advance the soap-opera element of the plot. Meanwhile, the city blows up because the nuke was in a warehouse. Jack, his wife, her lover, and the terrorist die, the terrorist feeling pleased that he managed to avoid being tortured in his last moments before his official martyrdom.)

Why keep all these people deteriorating in a prison, without hope for a trial, and subjecting them to routine torture? Or, worse, do so without even bothering to put together files on the individual prisoners? Yes, *The Washington Post* reported on January 25 that the Obama administration discovered from the Bushies that the U.S. government hadn't even kept comprehensive files on many of the Guantánamo prisoners. Hard as it may be to believe, the Bush administration seems to have needed these prisoners to languish indefinitely to reinforce the idea that, in a world teeming with terrorists, only this administration had the guts to just lock them up and throw away the key.

As unpleasant an assertion as this may be, let's face it: Republicans have a symbiotic relationship with terrorism and have come to rely on it to support their two major goals, which are getting elected and distracting the public from Republicans' raiding of the public treasury for corporate giveaways. I hate to say this, because then I feel like I'm feeding the delusions of 9/11 Truthers who want to believe that Bush either planned the attacks of 9/11 or let them happen to bolster the Republican agenda. But I can believe that Bush was a major-league opportunistic sleaze without my having to buy into conspiracy theories.

Right-wingers didn't have to invent communism or fake communist misbehavior to exploit it ruthlessly for political gain. And ruthlessly exploit it they did. (In the 1960s, Democrats did, too—then it blew up in their face in the shape of Vietnam.) Without communism, Reagan would be rightly remembered as a doddering old fool who put flowers on the gravestones of S.S. officers, claimed to have fought in WWII (when he hadn't), and made up bizarre lies about how women on welfare drive around in Cadillacs on the public dime. Instead, he gets to be remembered as the man who magically brought down the Berlin Wall by pointing at it.

It was obvious to any honest observers that Bush and his supporters hadn't wanted 9/11 but did capitalize eagerly on the threat of terrorism, starting the second Bush stepped on the World Trade Center's remains with a bullhorn in his hand. Terrorist enemies were the perfect enemy! Terrorism meant you could give up dealing with hated Democrats by trying to argue against them; now all you had to do was call them pussies and imply they want to throw out the red carpet to anyone wishing to bomb your house. This was an enemy so powerful that we the voters simply must set aside our need for jobs, health care, and justice to prevent what little we were permitted to keep from blowing up due to a random terrorist attack right in our very own neighborhoods. Yes, even if we lived in Des Moines, but even more if we lived in a swing state.

Of course, most wannabe terrorists don't have access to nuclear weapons, or many weapons at all, besides the box cutters the 9/11 terrorists used to hijack planes, which are now pretty much guaranteed to never work again, unless someone happens to hijack a plane full of people who haven't heard the story of United flight 93, and no one would gamble on that. Painting a loosely organized group of criminals as supervillains who outstrip all supervillains before them would take more than waving your hands around and screaming. You'd need some high-dollar and genuinely well-written, entertaining propaganda, like *24*. You'd need an endless stream of right-wing writers and pundits explaining how this was like World War II, except with an even more powerful and frightening enemy.

And you'd need an administration willing to violate the Geneva Convention, torture prisoners, suspend habeas corpus, spy on its own citizens, and have secret prisons to drive home the message that we live in times so crazy that basic decency itself had to be put on hold. Not everyone bought it, of course. Plenty of people stood up and pointed out that if civil rights could survive the fight against fascism, they could sustain the fight against a few fanatics hanging out in the desert, making videos. But the tactics worked as well as they needed to—convinced that only the Bush administration had the guts to flout the law on the hunt for the nefarious terrorist threat, a slim majority of Americans elected Bush in 2004.

Of course, in the long run, it looks like overreacting to a threat in a blatantly self-serving manner might not have been the best long-term strategy for Republicans. Or maybe not. If the economy had survived the assaults the Bush administration laid on it, maybe we'd still see people voting for Jack Bauer to torture the new communists on TV.

OUR NEWEST
EXCUSE NOT TO
Take Care of Business
at Home

A month into Obama's administration, the Pew Research Center published a report showing that 50 percent of Americans approved of Obama's performance in the mythological War on Terror, 21 percent disapproved, and 29 percent had the courage to admit that they had no real opinion on the subject. If more people were willing to admit the truth, that 29 percent would have been much higher. It's not that Obama avoided the group of issues collected in the popular mind under the word "terrorism," or in the friendlier, warmer terms conservatives prefer: "terror" or even "terra." He set the wheels in motion to shut down the hell on Earth known as Gitmo, reasserted some horrible things Bush did, and shut down other horrible things Bush did.

But the nation was in the grip of an economic crisis, and the only people who cared about this stuff were political junkies. Conservatives who had insisted a few years before that terrorism was a threat to humanity that made the Nazis look like amateurs couldn't even be bothered to do more than offer a few half-baked defenses of the Iraq War before diving right into bug-eyed screaming about the brand-new threat to life itself: social spending that might actually help people not starve to death. The rest of the country also had all its attention on the collapsing economy and attempts to save it and didn't have time to worry too much about terrorism.

Apparently, it takes near total economic collapse for Americans to pay attention to problems at home when sexy, semimythical foreign threats are dangled in front of them as a distraction.

Which isn't to say that the events of 9/11 were anything short of horrific. In fact, it's safe to say that it's the single greatest crime ever committed in American history, and I challenge anyone who claims she felt anything but utter shock when it happened. But it was, at the end of the day, a major crime and not an act of war (which would have required an army behind it, instead of a handful of box cutters) or a harbinger of the end of civilization itself. The Bushies sold it to us as these things, asking us to believe ridiculous things like "A man in a cave with a ragtag group of religious extremists presents a bigger threat than the well-armed, well-maintained Axis powers did in World War II." And they did it so they could have a shot at being the real threat to our civilization, unimpeded by troublesome voters.

Terrorism distracted us from our real problems right through the 2004 election, and the Bushies wielded it so obviously that many liberals who saw it for what it was thought they were losing their minds. In the days running up to the election, the Bush administration invented the Homeland Security Advisory System, a silly color-coded chart that tells us if we have a yellow or an orange chance of being murdered by Islamic extremists. And by "chance you'll get murdered by Islamic extremists," the administration meant, "chance that Bush's stupidity and evil might actually cost him the election." But it felt stupid and paranoid to say that out loud, even though yellow switched to orange and back depending on Bush's poll standings. I remember mentioning on my blog that I feared the threat levels reflected the polls more than they reflected any real threat, and every time, I regretted saying it, because a bunch of conservatives screamed that I was paranoid, and I worried that they might have a point.

I'll bet that as you read this passage, though, you're fumbling around in your brain and going, *Oooooooh, yeah. I remember those yellow/orange panic-button news alerts on the TV. What did happen to them? Yeah, they did disappear pretty promptly after Bush won the election in 2004.* Oh, they're still around, and you might occasionally see the charts in airports. But they don't show up on the news, and I'm not sure that anyone's actually bothered to change the level since November 2004. If the Bush administration hadn't come up with the damn thing as a campaign ploy (with the side benefit of creating a few no-work-necessary jobs for its buddies), then the administration's behavior would have been indistinguishable from that of a group of people who do something like that for no other reason than to scare a bunch of naive people into voting away their futures. Which is what nearly happened.

Terrorism got Bush elected in 2004, and he immediately tried to take your Social Security savings and put it into the stock market. And considering how well the market did in the years after the failed Bush privatization scheme, I'm certain a large number of senior citizens are eating hamburgers with glee, grateful that they aren't dog food. Of course, that large infusion of Social Security cash might have kept the market afloat for another year or two—just long enough for a few more insanely wealthy people to cash out before the bottom fell out and you started your dog-food retirement fund.

People consider Hurricane Katrina a turning point for the Bush administration because it nicely demonstrated the administration's incompetence and utter lack of concern for most Americans. But I tend to think it was a turning point for a very specific reason: It showed to all but the most stalwart Bush supporters that all Bush's posturing about how only

Daddy Republicans could protect us from massive catastrophe resulting in thousands of deaths—i.e., Republicans' only argument in favor of themselves—was pure, unadulterated bullshit. Bush couldn't stop a hurricane from killing a bunch of people, even though he a) saw it coming and b) had the procedures on hand (evacuation) to save lives—two advantages he would not have had if there had been a terrorist attack. It's sort of like finding out that your security guards left the door unlocked and let strangers walk up and borrow their guns.

Nightmares of terrorist attacks drove many Americans to the polls to vote against their own interests in 2004, and of the many bitter ironies that situation brought up, the largest may be that most of them had no chance, even the remotest chance, of getting killed in a terrorist attack. New Yorkers and District of Columbia residents saw through Bush's bullshit and voted for Kerry. In fact, if terrorists ever lucked out again and pulled off another big attack, and if they didn't hit either of those cities, they'd probably still hit a major metropolitan area. And even in the red states, all those cities voted for Kerry.

If you read the electoral map's reaction to the terrorist threat we heard so much about, you'd think radical Muslim terrorists had a hard-on for suicide-bombing strip malls out in the Kansas exurbs. The grand Obama win that swept in many supposedly solid red states, like Indiana, will be analyzed for decades to come. The consensus seems to be that economic factors cinched Obama's victory. Without disputing this, I'd like to add that perhaps the rural red-state voters began to wake up and realize that feed silos wouldn't actually be doused with anthrax and suicide bombers wouldn't set themselves off in the local Wal-Mart, and they felt free to pay attention to the threats that actually threatened them.

AIRPORT SECURITY:
Drama-Queen Behavior
to Keep Us in Line

Flying a lot will make the most forgiving, liberal-minded, empathetic human being despair for the human condition. Not when you suffer bureaucracy to buy your ticket, not when you check your bags and pay a fee, not when you board the plane after long delays, not even when some asshole next to you tries to chat you up during the whole flight. All this can be forgiven by an empathetic, kind-hearted liberal. But post-9/11, the security checkpoint went from being a mere formality to being a ritualistic sacrifice of your time and dignity to the gods of homeland security.

Most people who work security checkpoints don't want to make your day hard for you, but, as with every profession, there will always be a few who take their job and its ego-stroking possibilities way too seriously. Fly enough, and you can see these people coming. It's the guy yelling out the rules over and over, glaring at anyone he thinks might be weaker than he is, and just generally itching to search someone. I react to these types the same way I react to creepy old men trying to get my attention in public—fold into myself, try to look nonthreatening, and get through it with as little trouble or interaction as possible. But those who get off on exploiting the rules to harass people tend to tell you quite a bit about the point behind the rules. Indeed, the bullies seem to be the only people doing the job as the Bush administration imagined it when it first laid down the new security rules at airports.

See, airport security doesn't really do much to make us safer, but it goes a long way toward cowing us and training us to accept routine humiliation and invasions of privacy by the government. The more dramatic, the better. Given the choice between making people take off some articles of clothing, even just shoes, and taking simpler measures that might actually do more to keep us safe, it seems the former wins out every time. Part of the reason is that making you take off your shoes is cheaper than equipping every airport with a pressure chamber to make sure that suitcases on planes don't have pressure-sensitive bombs in them (a measure taken by Israel), but mostly it's because the Bushies had a collective instinct about how to bully and cow people most effectively. The high drama at airport security—getting yelled at because you forgot to take your plastic bag out of the suitcase, having security officials glare at your laptop as if it's a ticking bomb, pushing some buttons on your cell phone to prove that it's really a cell phone, or whatever fresh hell they come up with to annoy you—treads that line between being annoying and being truly offensive enough for people to revolt.

Of all the airport security rules, the one that causes the most consternation is the rule about having no liquids in bottles that hold more than three ounces, and stuffing them all in a plastic bag that you're then supposed to remove from your suitcase and put in a separate tub so that everyone can know that you can't travel without Preparation H, or that you really do wear that much makeup. Almost everyone who travels much at all has stories about having to relinquish cherished items to security to get to the plane— bottles of wine, expensive perfumes or cosmetics, and even a tub of hair gel that's been discontinued.

But all this embarrassment and loss doesn't do much to keep us safe, according to security experts. Joe Trento, who wrote the book *Unsafe at Any Altitude,* explained that the three-ounce rule wouldn't adequately prevent terrorists from combining their bottles of explosive liquid once they were onboard a plane. And in fact, much smaller amounts could be used to kill or maim airline staff—as we all know from 9/11, hijackers can take over a plane with a few measly box cutters.

My favorite part of the liquids rule might be when a security guard notices someone with a bottle of water, instructs the person to drink it before she goes through security, and then forces her to throw out what's left. You'd think that the fact that the person takes big gulps of whatever liquid is in the bottle would be solid evidence that it isn't statistically likely to be nitromethane. But if the guard considered this and let the person keep her bottle of water, then she wouldn't have a reason to spend $2.50 on another bottle of water at the airport gift shop.

Ostensibly, the whole process is supposed to catch would-be terrorists, but functionally, it makes you feel exposed and kind of helpless. This really came home to me when I flew to San Francisco for a conference. When I opened my suitcase in my hotel, I found a neat little card right next to my vibrator that indicated that the Transportation Security Administration had searched my bag. I stood there for a moment, feeling genuinely paranoid about what the TSA would do with me now that it has on record that I occasionally fly with marital aids, when I'm not married. Mind you, I live in Texas, where selling such things could land a person in jail until recently, so my concerns about being marked as a troublemaker were, if a tad overblown, rooted in a realistic understanding of the score. But I shrugged it off, washed my vibrator, and used the whole occasion as an amusing cocktail-party anecdote.

Then it occurred to me that this is, if not the intention of this sort of search tactic, the function of it. If we all feel a little watched and all feel like we engage in behaviors (like masturbation or criticizing the government) that have a quasi-legal status, then we begin to have an itching fear in the back of our minds. We start to worry about whether or not it's safe to have airport security possibly recording what we have in our luggage—and I often have reading material that marks me as quite unlikely to be a Republican—but we don't think about it too much, because we don't want to be paranoid. Even though we know that the Bush administration signed off recording people's phone calls, Internet behavior, and library histories.

Indeed, the most likely explanation for the unnecessary histrionics at airport security is that they're part of the "frog in boiling water" strategy of introducing a stronger police state. The idea is that you don't toss a frog straight into boiling water, or he'll jump out. Nor do you set up a Big Brother monitor in every home, or your citizens will revolt. Instead, you slowly turn up the heat, giving the frog/citizens time to adjust to it, until you eventually reach the same goal. Since airport security represents mostly an opportunity for mild embarrassment, dirty socks, and wasted time, it doesn't seem like as big a deal as the government's setting up a warrantless wiretapping program. Which means that when the warrantless wiretapping program was exposed a few years down the road, it didn't seem as alarming as it would have in a world where we were permitted to enter the gating area with our shoes proudly tied.

Of course, all this is Bush-league stuff, pardon the pun. Surely now that Obama's in office, we don't have to worry about this stuff anymore, right?

Sadly, no. The whole thing illustrates why you don't want to give a bunch of politicians unnecessary power for the sole purpose of power tripping, because they're generally loath to give it back. Why? They like power,

DON'T ASSUME
Democrats Are Our Friends

— 66 ! 99 —

After seven years of living with the Bush administration's justifying everything imaginable with the War on Terror (you can imagine some Republicans caught cheating on their wives probably even tried to blame it on a greater need for national security), America seemed pretty well sick of it. There are many reasons why we threw the bums out and elected a Democratic president and huge Democratic majorities in both houses of Congress, but being sick to the teeth of the word "terror" probably ranked among the top five.

Too bad for us, thinking that simply changing parties with a mandate for changing policy would result in an *actual* change. But for a short time, even this cynic thought maybe President Obama would do the right thing and stop the outrageous human-rights abuses the Bush administration set in motion. Didn't a memo calling to expedite the trials and releases of the prisoners of Guantánamo Bay reach the lawyers and judges working in the Cuban outpost before Barack and Michelle Obama had finished dancing at the inauguration ball?

Sadly, my cynicism turned out to be the proper response. The ugly truth of life is that once power is given, it's hard to take away. The second truth is that Democrats are little babies who are so terrified of looking like wimps that they don't realize that they could take Rush Limbaugh out in the street and beat him with a hose, and he'd still go on the radio—after he'd made a miraculous, Oxytocin-related recovery—and call Democrats a bunch of pussies. The third truth is that everyone who inherits a war tends to think that instead of ending it, he could just do a better job of winning it than his predecessor did. Call it the Dick-Swinging Principle, and it infects all politicians, even those who don't have dicks, due to their hunger for competition and victory.

As I write this, Obama's promises to get us the fuck out of Iraq and to figure out what to do with all the illegally held detainees at Guantánamo have both turned out to be big, fat lies. Oh, I'm sure Obama intended to do the right thing when he started off, but the Three Principles of Eternal Democratic Suckitude tend to defeat all comers, and even our charmingly self-assured president was no match for them.

This leaves us with precious few options. Voting for Republicans is out. Voting for third parties is basically voting for Republicans. Writing stern letters to your representatives might help, but since this war was basically conducted outside of congressional authority, it tends to persist no matter what they do. You could become an anarchist and declare the state permanently corrupt, but you're probably not going to go live in the woods in protest, because that would make you seem kind of silly. Saying, "C'est la vie" and living your life as if politics is beneath you might be the sanest choice, but it feels immoral.

You're left with being perpetually pissed about it and reading Daily Kos. But don't despair—Daily Kos might actually be a useful way to fight the system. Every election cycle, it does a better job of funding liberal candidates to run against conservative-coddling Democrats and making it clear that we want a genuinely progressive Democratic agenda. So far, that's meant largely that Daily Kos has run Joe Lieberman out of the Democratic Party—though he's not yet out of the Senate, it's a start. And it's better than trying to learn to wipe your ass with pinecones because you can't stand to be part of this imperialist system any longer.

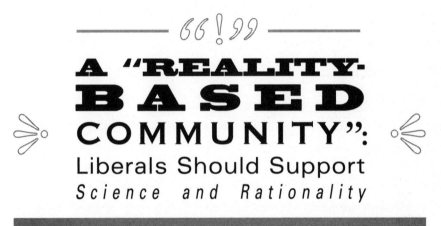

A "REALITY-BASED COMMUNITY":
Liberals Should Support
Science and Rationality

CHAPTER NINE

IF SCIENCE IS SO RATIONAL,
How Can It Be Political?

When I started writing this book, I knew I wanted it to have a section dedicated to the liberal obligation to defend science right alongside human rights, freedom, economic justice, and good rock 'n' roll. But doing so means coming into direct conflict with the more high-minded ideas about how science is apolitical and ideally objective, free of ideology and dedicated to truths instead of spin. All these things about science are true, which just means that, like all good and pure things (motherhood, baseball, and sex), it needs dirty, nasty political types to protect and defend it, to sully ourselves so it can survive.

That, and I like science and skepticism and need an excuse to write about them.

In truth, a decade ago, the idea of defending science from a specifically liberal perspective wouldn't have made much sense at all. Scientists may be nerdier and more atheistic than the public at large, but they're still a diverse group, with plenty of Republicans and aggressively apolitical types in their ranks. Add to that the above-it-all nature of science, and you have, if not a solid argument against this liberal defense, at least an intimidating obstacle.

Then the Bush administration unleashed its fury on reality itself, attacking it anytime it conflicted with the administration's agenda, which was most of the time. And if reality-based assertions like "People don't like it when you bomb their houses" and "Flushing the economy down the toilet hasn't worked in the past, so it shouldn't now" couldn't pass the no-reality zone, bona fide scientific assertions didn't stand a chance. The Bush administration and other conservative Republicans cracked down on any and all science they found politically incorrect, from stem cell research to global warming to evolutionary theory to the safety of over-the-counter emergency contraception to proven sex-education techniques to pretty much any environmental claims. Science funding unrelated to weapons development saw greater dangers, and actual scientists working in agencies like the FDA resigned rather than deal with anti-science religious wackos who controlled the agencies under Bush.

The whole thing really brought the science gap between liberals and conservatives to the forefront. Liberals began to call themselves the "reality-based community," after journalist Ron Suskind caught a Bush aide dismissing people who based their decisions on reason and evidence as members of the "reality-based community," a group of stubborn people who want their decisions to reflect reality, not wishful thinking. The evangelical movement, with its obstinate beliefs in demonic possession and creationism, took more and more control of the Republican Party, highlighting only the differences between the two sides. Every battle pitched over science—over stem cells, emergency contraception, even the evidence fixing around the possibility of weapons of mass destruction in Iraq—put liberals in the camp of science and rationality, and conservatives in that of fantasies and magical thinking.

And then there was global warming, which grew tremendously as an issue, due in no small part to the hard work of former vice president Al Gore.

Given a figurehead of the global-warming movement to hate, right-wingers glommed on and started to suck the bile teat like there was no tomorrow. The hate just helped redefine Gore: He stopped being the barely tolerable centrist Democrat of old and became an icon of liberal rationality and humor, beloved by all but a few who still remembered voting for Nader and weren't willing to take that back. Before *An Inconvenient Truth* had finished its run in the theaters, Gore's role as a sober-minded (if twinkle-eyed) liberal rationalist who put evidence (no matter how inconvenient) before ideology had solidified in the public mind.

I, for one, fully support my liberal, rationalist masters. It's hard to go wrong with scientific rationality as a baseline for your belief system and decision-making strategies. Reality, as Stephen Colbert said, has a well-known liberal bias. We find, with practice, that dedicating ourselves to scientific rationality becomes less scary over time. If you fear tripping over a bunch of inconvenient truths that will screw up your worldview, you'll discover that you have little to fear. Plus, evidence so obviously trumps fantasy that even fantasists try to pass off their nonsense in scientific skins to give it more credibility. (First exhibit: "intelligent design.")

Alas, one of the major obstacles for us liberals who want to wield more political muscle in attempts to defend science against the forces of anti-intellectualism, fantastic thinking, and wishful thinking is the cadre of fantasists, anti-intellectuals, and wishful thinkers on the left. So, while most of this book is aimed at building up liberals and tearing down conservatives, I have to spend some time dwelling on some anti-scientific thinking among Democrats that is preventing from us from moving to the next level. I won't waste too much energy taking on chakras and detoxing, but some anti-science beliefs have taken root in the left, and they have to go. It's for our own good.

SHOTS BEFORE
YOU'RE SICK
Don't Seem Right

The bulk of anti-science ideological wanking comes from the right—claims that the earth has abundant resources, that there's no global warming, that AIDS is caused by butt sex and not a virus, that evolutionary theory is a conspiracy concocted to make you personally look stupid. This means that liberals, as I've mentioned before, are in a perfect position to appoint ourselves the guardians of scientific inquiry against assaults from ignorant ideologues and reap all the benefits of looking honorable and intellectual because of it. Unfortunately, we may have to do a little housecleaning before we can wear that mantle.

I propose starting with anti-vaccination hysteria. Anti-vaccination fanatics, known increasingly as the pro-disease squad, have managed to sculpt arguments that sound like they came from the *Selling Things to Whole Foods–Loving Yuppies Handbook*. Celebrity granola heads and vaccination opponents such as Jenny McCarthy insinuated that regular childhood vaccinations were full of vaguely defined toxins and toyed with more boldly stating that the autism epidemic was caused by vaccination. (Most sober-minded assessments explain the rise in autism cases by the presence of better screening methods that caught most of the cases that would have gone undiagnosed in the years before.) Anti-vaccination hostility exploded after Dr. Andrew Wakefield published a research study in *The Lancet* in 1998 linking vaccinations to autism. With that small and highly contested amount of evidence to back it, the anti-vaccination frenzy exploded among the left-leaning yuppie set, pushing the noncompliance rates in some charter schools in Southern California to around 50 percent. A measles outbreak in San Diego soon followed, with the Centers for Disease Control and Prevention flagging places like Whole Foods and Trader Joe's as hot spots for potential infection. In the U.K., health authorities declared that vaccination resistance had returned measles to an endemic status.

In retrospect, it makes sense why the granola moms would ignore all studies that showed, over and over again, that there was no link between childhood vaccinations and autism. First of all, anti-vaccination activists claimed they were for only "green" vaccinations, and the word "green" can pull interest from about 25 percent of the organic-food set without the activists' even having to put forward a minimal effort to define "green." (It was all a lie—while demanding green vaccinations, the anti-vaccination set had already started to measure its success in the number of children who went unvaccinated.) But mostly the anti-vaccination rhetoric fed the yuppie trend of hypercontrolling, pseudonaturalistic parenting. When you make a full-time job out of monitoring every bite of food that goes into your kid's mouth because you're overreacting to the (admittedly disgusting) poor nutritional habits that dominate the country, it becomes easy to start convincing yourself that you have complete control over the situation. You believe disease is a big deal only for parents whose kids eat less organic food, and that you can, through mother love and the help of Whole Foods, provide all the preventive medicine your kid needs.

In case there was any doubt that this motivation fueled much of the anti-vaccination paranoia, consider this: Actress Jenny McCarthy is probably the nation's foremost anti-vaccination spokesperson. She also claimed to have cured her son of autism through nutrition. The common thread is that Jenny McCarthy knows more than you stupid doctors. God help us if she decides she knows more about structural engineering than people who actually know what they're doing, and decides to go into bridge building.

Plus, hostility to vaccinations gives people a simple way to oppose the drug industry without having to learn anything about it or its complexities. If you assume the most selfless thing it does is not only evil, but superevil, you don't have to worry about expending the energy to learn what parts of Big Pharma are good, what parts are bad, and what parts are a mixed blessing.

There's no doubt that autism is really scary. The problem is that the single study by Dr. Wakefield wasn't just disproven by subsequent research, it was also exposed as a total fraud. The *Sunday Times of London* found that Dr. Wakefield changed and misreported his findings to establish a link that wasn't there between vaccines and autism.

The *Times*'s exposé of Andrew Wakefield caused pro-science activists to celebrate prematurely. Blogger David Gorski declared on the blog Science-Based Medicine in February 2009 that anti-vaccinationists were facing a bad upcoming year, now that their last thread to reality had been cut. I wished I could be as optimistic as he was, but I knew that the chances of anti-vaccination activists' relenting even the slightest bit under a wave of scientific evidence were less than nothing.

Despite hailing from the other side of the political spectrum, anti-vaccination activists remind me of nothing so much as anti-choice activists. They have their issue, and it's tied to their own feelings of purity and loss of control, and even though their enthusiasm for their respective causes (raising the rate of communicable diseases, eliminating sex for pleasure) doesn't make sense by any rational measure, they won't give up. In fact, the very irrationality of their positions tends to make them adopt the bunker conspiracy–theorist mentality: They are the only ones who understand the truth, and they're railing against the rest of us, who are "blinded" by science and reason.

Anti-choicers aren't deterred by science. If anything, they see it as another obstacle to overcome in their pure mission of wiping nonprocreative sex off the planet. They claim that abortion causes depression and breast cancer, and no number of studies disproving this theory will ever cause them to budge from these convenient opinions. I saw no reason to think that anti-vaccination activists would act any differently in the face of overwhelming evidence against them. If anything, they'll just show the know-it-alls that they can win even without science on their side. It was shortly after Wakefield was exposed that I first heard of anti-vaccination activists' tracking their success by numbers of kids left unvaccinated, and that was when I knew that my prediction was likely right—they're just going to be more adamant now that they've been proven wrong.

To say that anti-vaccination activists come from the left isn't exactly right, though. Many radical movements—some that are harmless to actively good (organic food), some that are harmful but probably not so much that they should be interfered with (homeschooling), and some that are plain nutty (incoherent hostility to modernism)—fold into each other on the left and the right. And left and right found each other when it came to a specific vaccination called Gardasil. Merck had developed it to fight the human papillomavirus (HPV) that causes, among other things, cervical cancer, and, of course, the right wing blew up in fury. After all, HPV is a sexually transmitted disease, albeit one so common that most adults will have it at some point, and so preventing the disease meant women would suffer that much less for being dirty, dirty whores. True, the disease is so common that many women who get it do so during missionary sex within the context of a monogamous marriage, but someone probably got off without getting pregnant, so suffering needs to happen—end of story.

This is usually not a mode of thinking you associate with the left. But ideological hostility to science makes for a strange bedfellow, and before you knew it, leftists and even feminists were making noises about how bad Gardasil was, and they were echoing right-wing language to do so. The moment that caused me the greatest indigestion was when I heard a bona fide feminist joke that HPV isn't that contagious for *everyone* (just for sluts—nudge, nudge), so she didn't see why universal vaccination was such a big deal.

That's the danger of embracing ideology over boring old scientific evidence. (Which isn't to say you should roll over for everything labeled "scientific"—there's a skill to telling good science from bad. But vaccinations have good science behind them.) All roads lead to wingnuttery. You may think you're above hinting that cervical cancer is what you get for fucking around, but if you spend enough time with anti-vaccination paranoids, that's the road you're on. Which is exactly why liberals need to make supporting the sciences central to our agenda.

JESUS AND/OR YOUR STAR SIGN
Want You to Be a Millionaire

If you ever want to see a rationalist tear her hair out, merely mention the bestseller *The Secret* to her. This book by Rhonda Byrne was trumpeted by Oprah Winfrey and sold millions of copies, all based on a theory that you can magically make good things happen in your life just by thinking about them. (And that if you think about negative things, magic will bring you illness and misfortune.) Reasonable people can immediately see the major flaws in this theory, though it's hard to pick between the most glaring ones. Do you go with "But bad things happen to upbeat people"? Do you point out that it's physically impossible to manipulate the world with imaginary "energies" that you control with your brain? Do you try to prove how stupid this all is by humming "Walking on Sunshine" over your lottery tickets and continuing not to win? Or do you do what most of us do, and decide to ignore the whole thing as a harmless, self-contained fad that has no bearing on how people actually live their lives?

Unfortunately, if you choose the last option, you're deluding yourself about a definite and unavoidable cultural shift in America toward this sort of magical thinking. And New Agers hardly have cornered the market on theories about how to bring wealth and well-being into your life through the power of wishful thinking; fundamentalist Christians also saw the appeal of this kind of thinking and latched on to it, developing what's called prosperity theology—the belief that if you're a good enough Christian, then God will make you wealthy and healthy and probably make your romantic relationships sexually and emotionally fulfilling. Enormous churches, especially with elaborate television-evangelism components, push this nonsense about how being rich and being good go hand in hand. Between the New Agers and the Christian nuts, the power of wishing over doing is something that millions upon millions of Americans are embracing.

The Secret and prosperity theology have as much crystalline elegance as pure bullshit could ever hope to have. Whatever happens to be going on right now with you just proves that these theories work: If you're doing well, you can pin it on the times you got out of bed the first time the alarm went off, had optimistic thoughts, and refrained from masturbating while thinking about your hot neighbor doing your spouse in front of you. But should something bad happen—such as your spouse's *actually* doing that hot neighbor—then it's your fault for being bad or having negative thoughts. Sure, you didn't masturbate to the image, but you still considered it, didn't you? That was enough, wasn't it? Since purging yourself completely of negativity or sinfulness is technically impossible, there's always evidence that you brought your own misfortune on yourself.

That's all too bad, you're surely thinking, but what does it have to do with liberalism? Well, liberals ought to be wary of all nonsense-based thinking, because it encourages the sort of disdainful relationship with reality that softened up Americans to think things like, *Sure, creationism is as good as evolutionary theory,* and *Maybe we can wish hard enough and teenagers will quit fucking,* and, of course, *I believe Saddam Hussein was behind 9/11, so he was!*

But more than that, the prevalence of Americans running from reality and hiding in such preposterous fantasies should concern us. Turning to
prayer and positive thinking is what people do when they don't think that
actual action makes any difference in their lives. They aren't wrong about
this: Various studies have shown that Americans have less class mobility than
people in Europe, even though we won't formally admit that we have classes,
as much of Europe does. You're not going up, you're always worried about
going down, and you don't have the language to talk about these concerns—
and then Oprah Winfrey or some televangelist tells you that you can quit
wasting your energy striving and worrying, and instead just start praying
and thinking good thoughts, and quit sinning. Of course it's seductive. It's
like playing the lottery, but you don't even have to buy a ticket, much less
sing any '80s pop hits over it.

GLOBAL WARMING
Is Not Controversial

Open any mainstream news story about global warming, and prepare to flinch at the word "controversial." Or maybe not. Maybe you, like most Americans, have seen the issue portrayed as a scientific controversy so often that you don't even question if it's a scientific controversy, just as medieval people whose lives were completely dominated by the church never had cause to wonder if there even was a Jesus. But the idea that global warming is controversial at all is another example of how the skittish media, in an effort to appear fair 'n' balanced, adds a lie to a truth, divides by two, and comes up with a half-truth to pass off to the public.

It seems that no amount of reality can penetrate the media's need to balance truth with lies offered by right-wingers who will defend corporate polluters past the point of being forced to suck directly on an exhaust pipe until they can feel the tumors growing. Not that the scientific community hasn't tried like hell to fight back. Report after report, committee after committee, scientific society after scientific study—all agree that global warming is real. Nothing dissuaded the skittish mainstream media from positioning the issue as "controversial," but some progress in convincing the public was made when *Science* magazine gathered up 928 of the most important studies on the issue in 2004, and found that all of them agreed that global warming is real and none disagreed with the evidence demonstrating that it's man-made.

Then Al Gore came out with a movie, and as we all know, a single movie can do more to a culture than all the books published in that year put together. *An Inconvenient Truth* had really cool charts and lifts, and it had a human-interest angle, and it's just hard to argue with those things. The public started to care a bit more. But the mainstream media refused to drop the "controversial" label, scared to death of being accused of bias by openly biased right-wing sources that will deny global warming's reality until their brains literally cook past the point where they can speak.

To be fair, there are some controversies regarding global warming. Scientists argue bitterly over whether or not it will kill us all or merely create an apocalyptic, *Mad Max*–esque scenario involving desert shootouts in cars run on solar panels and fear. Or if it's going to be just a slow burn, where reduced resources due to flooding in some places and drought in others cause international war that is even more devastating in terms of loss of life. There are debates over how much starvation to expect, and how quickly we'll see flooding due to ice caps' melting. There are also debates about whether or not the increased hurricane rate is absolutely due to global warming, or if it's just a warning that we're lucky to get. But when mainstream media sources say global warming is "controversial," they're referring to whether or not it exists and is man-made.

Arguing with a global-warming denialist could be compared to banging your head against a wall, but that really exaggerates the pain of banging your head against a wall. As someone who can't resist trying it, I highly recommend avoiding it, unless you personally did research on one of the 928 studies that shored up the near impossibility that denialists are right. The first thing a denialist will do is exploit the fact that you're not a scientist, and try to make this a debate about your authorities versus his authorities. Without my going into tedious detail about the specifics, the way this works is that a handful of people with dubious scientific esteem—a handful (if even that many) of metereologists, mostly—have traded in on their tenuous authority for some cold, hard cash from industries with a vested interest in global-warming denialism, such as oil companies. That's all the denialist needs to turn the conversation from whether or not global warming is true to whether or not you can really say that 99 percent of the scientific community's opinions on it trump those of some weatherman from Canada.

I fell for this trap once, and it wasn't pretty. It got to the point where, after I pointed out that you can buy off 1 percent of anyone with the sort of cash that oil companies offer, I had to defend the very existence of research funding. No, I'm not kidding. This is the sort of slippery nonarguing and point dodging that average Americans learn from right-wing talk radio.

Me: So they found one sleazy Canadian weatherman who will say whatever they want him to for a check heavy with zeroes. This proves nothing but that oil companies are so screwed on this issue that they have to pay to play.

Denialist: Yeah, but all those scientists are dirty. They want global warming to be real so they can suck the government teat for more research money.

Me: Are you kidding? Are you actually comparing people who work for their money and have to go through a

painful grant-application process to someone who spouts
off bullshit for one hour a week and gets paid like he's a
fucking CEO?

Just kidding. That's what I should have said. What I did say was slightly different.

Me: (Sputters.) Do you really think that the entire enter-
prise of science is too corrupt to do anything right?

Smug Denialist: That's what happens when you let the
government give you money, instead of corporations.

Me: You really think corporations are more compelled to
be honest than universities? (Nervous collapse due to
inability to process delusions.)

Really, this dialogue nearly ruined my sister's wedding, so I do not recommend this approach under any circumstances. Debating the evil that lurks in 99 percent of scientists (compared with the 1 percent whose purity is rewarded only by fat corporate checks) is a losing strategy, because you can't actually peer into their souls and see if they have evil etched on them. And that's the point of the strategy, and why right-wing radio teaches it—it's always easier for right-wingers to argue on grounds that can't be proven definitively than on grounds where the evidence is just piled up against them.

Instead, stick to that magic number, 928. Scratch it on your brain, alongside the words "*Science* magazine" and "2004." That's what you need to know to argue your point without getting into a pointless debate about whether or not people who spend fifty to sixty hours a week in the classroom or doing research are lazy bastards sucking the government teat. Whenever a global-warming denialist brings up Canadian meteorologists who refute global warming or medical doctors who drive Hummers or anyone who seems kind of scientistlike, despite their willingness to engage in unscientific and immoral denialism, don't even engage the attack. Just state, "*Science* magazine collected all 928 major studies on global warming, and every single one found it to be real."

Your opponent, who will have no rebuttal, will slither and slide around and refuse to engage with you on the topic. Just firmly repeat the point: 928, *Science* magazine, 2004. Liberals often fear repetition; they see it as an insult to the intelligence of their audience, who heard them the first time. But remember, if you're dealing with a global-warming denialist, he and the people he listens to are the ones insulting his intelligence. He probably knows on some level that his tiny cadre of wingnut pseudoscientists is a group of well-paid liars. Your only job is to drive this idea home for him, by repeating that one talking point. Or wear him out before he wears you out. It's not ideal, but it's still preferable to banging your head against a wall.

BECOME A
POLITICAL
SKEPTIC
and Science Promoter

—— 66 ! 99 ——

Believe it or not, there's actually an entire political movement (based largely in the United States and Great Britain) dedicated to skepticism and promoting science and rationality. The problem is, the followers of this movement don't really consider themselves political, probably in no small part because they rely on a series of non-profit organizations that are explicitly nonpartisan to retain their tax-exempt status. Hey, we all gotta save money in a recession. But the ugly truth—one that's being embraced by science promoters the nation over—is that science and rationality are political issues, whether we like it or not.

And scientists do not like. As Chris Mooney and Sheril Kirshenbaum document in their book, *Unscientific America*, from about the 1950s until the Bush administration, scientists conducted themselves largely as creatures above the political fray, until the aggressively anti-science policies of the Bush administration forced more of them to get into the muck. Some found they have a taste for the muck, but for the rest, I think it would be best if the people out there who adore the muck freed them up to go back to the lab and research things that are more important than scoring partisan points. Like curing cancer.

That means you. After the Bush administration, science has become a partisan issue, with the American right increasingly kicking fits over the way reality impedes its goals on everything from global warming to sexual-health issues. And that means that those of us who care about the planet and its people more than we care about profits have a mission to embrace science and impress upon the public the need to pay attention to reality, rationality, and evidence when we're making policy decisions.

What you *can* do is bone up on your skepticism skills. There are tons of websites and podcasts out there covering how to be skeptical about things like homeopathy and hauntings, and how to understand what real science looks like versus fake science. Some of my favorites are Skepticblog, Skepchick, the Skeptics' Guide to the Universe, and Science-Based Medicine. Once you've sharpened your skills at evaluating these nonpolitical, bullshit claims, you can really start to attack right-wing (and, occasionally, left-wing) assaults on reality itself.

The best thing to practice with is global warming,

because the evidence in favor of it is so overwhelming, but the evidence against it is so amplified by very expensive megaphones. Calmly load yourself up with the damning fact that 928 out of 928 studies on global warming have indicated that it's real and likely caused by human beings, and calmly repeat this scientific fact to everyone who's like, "Yeah, well, I woke up this morning, and it wasn't that fucking hot." Once you're steady on your feet, you can start to expand your ability to use evidence and logic against bullshit and wishful thinking.

"!"
OR MAYBE
THE COLOR PURPLE:
The Red State/
Blue State Divide

CHAPTER TEN

SHOOTING BEER CANS
for Freedom

Recently, my friend and I were enjoying a microbrew at a local pub populated by the tattooed people of Austin, like the effete liberals we are, and my friend, who developed a minor obsession with Sarah Palin during her run for the vice presidential slot, mentioned seeing a bumper sticker he didn't quite understand on the back of a pickup truck the size of a house that said, simply, SARAH PALIN IS RIGHT ON TARGET.

His confusion stemmed from a simple problem: He'd always imagined that bumper stickers, at least those sporting some kind of slogan, were supposed to be funny. If so, was this supposed to be? It was entirely possible, my friend suggested, that the redneck behind the wheel was expressing some sort of wingnut "humor" that those blessed with a genuine funny bone might not quite understand. (This problem crops up a lot when I'm reading or listening to reactionaries attempt to be funny, especially if they're straying from the comfortable territory of making blatantly racist jokes.) Or was this some sort of elaborate act of performance art staged by a hipster who had graduated from merely wearing trucker hats and drinking Pabst Blue Ribbon to the next level of irony? My friend wanted my opinion.

"Sounds like an NRA thing to me," I said, drawing on my unhappily long history of associating with mean rednecks.

"Oh, duh, of course!" my friend replied, smacking his beer down for emphasis. "It was black on a yellow background. Of course it's some dumb gun-nut-redneck thing." Which meant that it was intended to be a joke, in the same way a bumper sticker that says GONE FISHIN' provides endless amounts of merriment.

Indeed, he should have been ashamed not to have picked up on this sooner, and I happily let him know it. We have shot beer cans off a fence together in our time, and he's liable to have guns strewn across his coffee table if you just happen to drop in for a visit. In other words, while we're both liberal elitists who make fun of our less open-minded redneck brethren, we don't do it because we're unfamiliar with redneck culture or even with the pleasure of shooting off guns. We do it because we know it so well.

For, as my gun-loving but liberal friends know, you can love shooting off guns, and you can dedicate a large portion of your home to storing them, but these things alone do not a gun nut make. To be blunt, to really be a gun nut, you have to have a near literal phobia of castration that you express through inculcating paranoid fears that a cadre of already castrated Democratic men, prodded by pitchfork-wielding feminists, is coming to take your guns. And then, when you don't have a means of defending yourself, they'll cut off your nutsack. The "god" and "gays" parts of the redneck-getting vote mantra of "God, Guns, and Gays" are just other variations on the emasculation fears. Gays merely existing is perilous to the nutsack, and god the sole protector. I shouldn't really have to explicate how abortion fits into the All about the Nutsack theory.

As a way to drum up votes, barely disguised fears of castration are second to none. If one party actually ran on a "cut off your nutsack" platform and the other ran on a "you get to keep your nutsack" platform, I suspect the latter party would get 99 percent of the vote, while the other 1 percent would be supported by a mix of people who can't fill out ballots properly, and perhaps one or two people that really have a problem with testicles. The issue is that there's not actually a "cut off your nutsack" party to run against, so Republicans have to claim there is one to lure the votes of the gullible. But they can't come right out and say that Democrats want your nuts, due to the fact that this might be an easier claim to disprove than all the whoppers McCain told about Obama, put together. Nut-chopping claims have to be made through implication and symbolism.

For the "guns = your nuts" claim to really work, however, you need a steady population of men who will eagerly make this connection, perhaps so quickly and subconsciously that they don't realize how insecure and emasculated their gun nuttery seems to outsiders. The NRA approaches these men with cartoonishly masculine movie stars like Charlton Heston and inelegant double entendres about removing guns from cold, dead hands, but this still doesn't explain why it finds such a large audience of anxious men ready to be reborn as gun nuts.

This is where this liaison between red culture and blue culture can't do much to help you. I have no idea why a certain set of white men seems to genuinely fear the imminent loss of cock and balls at the hands of John Kerry and Gloria Steinem. I'm sure their genitals are as firmly tied to their bodies through skin and muscle as those of more liberal gentlemen who do not fear the guns-then-genitals midnight snatching. Snickers about penis size seem like they might have a little more validity, but it doesn't make sense that merely living in a red community makes you more likely to have a small penis than living in a blue community does. Genetics seem the more obvious source of penis-size determination.

No, these levels of anxiety must have a source outside of a biological basis. People smarter than I am have concluded that the declining economic fortunes of the more conservative parts of the country have coincided with gains made by women, gays, and racial minorities. The stress of declining white-male privilege is exacerbated by economic problems, creating emasculation fears then exploited by reactionary groups like the NRA and, eventually, by the Republican Party. It all makes perfect sense, until you realize that they're still in a panic about a symbolic castration that no reasonable person could think is a real threat, and then you're back to square one with wondering how we got into this situation in the first place.

TRUE PATRIOTS
Eat Gravy

Austin, Texas—where I've stubbornly set down roots and refuse to move from—is well known as the cool part of Texas, an oasis of blue in a red state. But it has a lot in common with the rest of the state, in both the rural and the urban areas: Country-western music is popular, and cowboy hats can be worn without irony. Tex-Mex and BBQ dominate the local cuisine. People talk about the weather with an intensity that raises it above small talk. "All y'all's" is considered a legitimate phrase. (As in, "We need to get all y'all's ear protection before we start shooting cans off this here fence.") We consider "darlin'" a very modern-sounding endearment.

The differences are hard enough to deny, however, that Austin's directly rural and redneck-leaning suburbs have a uniquely strong hostility toward the sea of blue. We're seen as queer-coddling, dope-smoking, abortion-loving hippies. But for me, the real moment when I really understood the size of the gulf between Austin-ites and the rest of Texas was when my aunt came for a visit from a less sexy part of the state, and everywhere she went, she marveled at how *thin* everyone was, how *good-looking,* how *healthy.* In part, it's because it's such a young town. But I drove the other main reason home by taking her to a grocery store here, with its dazzling piles of fresh produce and bins full of whole grains that I hadn't even heard of until I moved to Austin. And that's without setting foot inside one of the city's many organic/hippie grocery stores, or pointing out how every restaurant we ate at had plenty of vegetarian options.

Call it the foodie gap, or yuppie pretentiousness, but either way, it's a real phenomenon that has the disturbing side effect of giving the privileged white people who live in red parts of the country more reason to think of themselves as bona fide populists, even if they're millionaires and the people they call the "liberal elite" are trying to figure out how they're going to pay for health insurance. (Case in point: Defeated VP hopeful Sarah Palin was rich as sin but acted like she experienced daily persecution at the hands of the socialist elite who made her, I don't know, shine shoes or something.) Food marks who is and isn't a member of the so-called "liberal elite" more all the time. As Laura Miller noted in *Salon:*

> It's no coincidence that when the conservative Club for Growth PAC produced its famous 2004 television commercial featuring an elderly couple telling Howard Dean to go "back to Vermont," two out of the seven outré practices Dean and his "left-wing freak show" were accused of involved comestibles: latte drinking and sushi eating.

It's clichéd but true to note that red voters' resentment of blue voters has not just a little hint of envy to it, as evidenced by my aunt's candid assessment of the health, beauty, and waistlines of the liberal elite that clog up the jogging paths in Austin. That the blues get to have the impressive, exotic foods, the tasty cheeses, the fancy wines, and the healthy organic food,

whereas the less fortunate parts of the country are brimming with chain restaurants and cheese that compensates for lack of quality with quantity stokes
these resentments. And now, as I've noted in other parts of the book, that
eating right has a moral angle, due to the environmental consciousness of it,
this gulf will only widen. In a sense, it really doesn't seem fair that the liberal
elite eats better and healthier *and* gets to feel morally superior about it.

Of course, the classic coping strategy for those burdened by the red
states' insecurity complex is to puff up the most depressing parts of their
cultural landscape as if they were touchstones. We see this in the right-
wing pundits who pretend they enjoy shopping at Wal-Mart, and in the
alarming increase in SUVs throughout the '90s into the early twenty-first
century. Really, you could graph it: SUV mileage went down as liberal
moral repulsion went up, and with it came the SUV fans' childish glee at
irritating the horrible liberal elite. It was fun for everyone until gas prices
hit $4 per gallon, and then the only people having fun were liberals who
got to say, "I told you so."

Now that food has not just a health component to it but also a political
and moral one, I fear we're going to see a wild surge in resentful wingnuts'
ordering their fries extra-super-large just to show the foodies, environmentalists, and health fanatics that wingnuts will sooner die of heart attacks
than allow some Obama-voting hippies to offer even the mildest suggestion about how to eat better. Will doubling the amount of gravy on your
chicken-fried steak become a "Fuck liberals!" comment, much as putting a
yellow-ribbon magnet on your car or perhaps even glowering at nubile (and
liberalish-looking) young women at the beach while drinking Budweiser
have been in the past?

Frankly, if you're a vegetarian liberal weenie, as I am, you know it's
already gotten bad. Get a grilled-cheese sandwich and a salad for lunch in the

wrong part of the country, and you find yourself in an unpleasant confrontation with someone who thinks that there's a whiff of communist atheism to the meat-free plate. But there's plenty of room for the situation to get worse.

Currently, most red-staters' willingness to piss off liberals by eating badly is mitigated by the near universal American desire to lose some weight already. A vegetable may be characterized as a pussified food, but it's also something that can occupy space in your stomach that you might otherwise feel compelled to fill with cheesecake. To make it worse, fat activism—which is a political movement pushing for better treatment and acceptance of fat people—is mostly a left-leaning phenomenon, so just eating poorly and getting fat to piss off the liberals puts you in another pro-liberal camp.

But right-wing nuts have had some practice in recent years handling the tension between the joy of annoying liberals and the need to avoid blatantly screwing themselves over. If nothing else, the people who bought liberal-annoying SUVs, only to find themselves facing insurmountable gasoline prices when the prices doubled, have weathered this storm. Of course, what most of them learned was that if you choose annoying liberals over taking care of yourself, you can't take it back. You can't sell that SUV when gas prices go up, and you can't just wish those artery clogs away if you decide to eat true patriot levels of fried food and gravy. Whether you prioritize annoying liberals or your own health has to be left up to individual discretion, and that's a painful reality for the side of the fence that puts the higher value on conformity.

WELFARE UNDERMINES
Our Jesus Recruitment

The economic crisis that started in late 2008 dominated the headlines, destroyed the lives of millions, depleted retirement savings, and left the population grasping, desperate, and afraid. According to *The New York Times* (December 13, 2008), the evangelical churches couldn't have been happier.

> *At the Life Christian Church in West Orange, New Jersey, prayer requests have doubled—almost all of them aimed at getting or keeping jobs.*
>
> *Like evangelical churches around the country, the three churches have enjoyed steady growth over the last decade. But since September, pastors nationwide say they have seen such a burst of new interest that they find themselves contending with powerful conflicting emotions—deep empathy and quiet excitement—as they re-encounter an old piece of religious lore:*
>
> *Bad times are good for evangelical churches.*

Democrats and liberals in general spend a lot of time worrying about how to get the churchy people to side with us instead of with the Republicans. *Surely,* we think, *people who believe in the Jesus who walked with lepers and consorted with prostitutes believe this is a Jesus who could convince his followers to embrace progressive economic positions.* We'd like to believe that members of the Christian right are in this only because they hate abortion and gays make them feel uneasy. But, we convince ourselves, since it's about god, guns, and gays for them, maybe they can be convinced there's some common ground on other issues. A better social safety net, for instance, would easily reduce the abortion rate, and maybe they can be convinced to care about that.

However, articles like the one I quoted above demonstrate why this tactic probably won't work. It may be true enough that the average pew-sitters in the fundamentalist-Christian movement feel drawn to it because thinking hurts them and they want other people to handle that responsibility. But the movement's leaders aren't so dumb—they realize that their power depends on the desperation of the people in the pews, and that they therefore need not just abortion bans and gay bashing, but the entire conservative package as well. They need policies that defund the working class and enrich the already wealthy at the expense of everyone else.

Barbara Ehrenreich noted in 2004 that megachurches were swooping in and filling the gap in services that our government should be providing but isn't.

A woman I met in Minneapolis gave me her strategy for surviving bouts of destitution: "First, you find a church." A trailer-park dweller in Grand Rapids told me that he often turned to his church for help with the rent. Got a drinking problem, a vicious spouse, a wayward child, a bill due?

Find a church. The closest analogy to America's bureau-cratized evangelical movement is Hamas, which draws in poverty-stricken Palestinians through its own miniature welfare state.

Of course, these services come at the price of conversion, or the semblance of it. A secular government offering services doesn't demand your conscience for you to eat, nor does it exploit desperation for recruitment purposes. In the area of social services alone, evangelical churches and the Republican Party have found a nice little partnership with each other. Republicans strip services and increase desperation. The churches pick up the desperate, feed them, and convince them that they need to vote for Republicans or they're going to hell. The Bush administration sweetened the deal by creating the concept of "faith-based funding," which allows evangelical Republican recruitment programs to offer welfare with a dose of Bible thumping on the taxpayer's dime.

It's not just welfare, either. As *The New York Times*'s article demonstrates, all sorts of conservative policies that screw people over drive them into the churches, hoping that god will magically make things better if they pray hard enough. Economic deregulation and regressive taxation structures send working people into an economic pit that does seem impossible to climb out of, and increase the number of people who just want to pray it away because they can't think of anything else to do. The Bush administration may not have wanted economic collapse, but its endless pursuit of any method to widen the gap between rich and poor made it happen anyway, and the evangelical churches benefited, which meant that the Republicans benefited.

Even though Obama and other Democrats saw sweeping wins in 2008, the Republicans did manage to hang on to a huge percentage of the electorate, mainly by sticking to socially conservative issues like abortion and gay marriage, issues that matter most to the evangelicals who flock in growing numbers to conservative churches because hard times make them desperate.

It's a great joke among liberals that the states where people preach the hardest about "family values"—the infamous red states—also have the worst family lives. Red states have higher rates of divorce, unplanned pregnancies, STDs, single-mother births—you name it, they suffer from it. As a resident of a solidly red state, I've witnessed this pattern firsthand: The harder we scream about families and children, the worse we do by them. Our education system is falling apart, and we seem determined to maximize teenage pregnancy.

Conservatives may characterize liberal policies as self-indulgent and decadent, but those same liberal policies lead to more peaceable family lives. Girls who get a better education and a more feminist upbringing delay childbirth. Couples who marry later and embrace equality divorce less. A better social safety net means fewer families that fall apart because of economic stress. Really, you can tell how decadent liberal society is by how happy it is. If nothing else, there's something ungodly about people who like the person they're married to. If god had intended marriage to be happy, he wouldn't have called it "wedlock."

If you look at how evangelical churches exploit hard times, it's easy enough to see that they actually benefit from divorce, teenage pregnancy, and other hardships, and therefore easy enough to also understand why they perceive all attempts to actually reduce these problems as a direct assault on their authority. The more chaotic people's home lives are, the more they willfully suspend disbelief and listen to preachers who seem to be using *Leave It to Beaver* as their main text more than they do the Bible. Megachurches learned a long time ago that they can hold audiences rapt by telling them tales of a world where Father knew best and no one ever fought or left each other. The Bible posits that the Garden of Eden was the actual Garden of Eden; your average megachurch suggests it was the 1950s suburbs. If we could shove gays in the closet and subjugate women, we could have perfection again.

If you were surprised by the evangelical reaction to Sarah Palin's pregnant teenage daughter, well, you shouldn't have been. If churches didn't want teenage girls getting pregnant, they wouldn't be telling them that the only acceptable form of birth control is abstinence, thereby guaranteeing that when they do fuck, they won't have any condoms on hand, much less hormonal contraception streaming through their systems. No one really believes you can stop kids from fucking. But what you *can* do is make the consequences of fucking as traumatic and life altering as possible. The problem with birth control, of course, is that it shows that "sinning" by having sex doesn't actually have to ruin your life. And once you know that, you don't need to go to church anymore and pray for perfection—which will never come—to have the better life that's right around the corner.

TURN YOUR RED STATE BLUE

— " ! " —

I live in Texas, as you have no doubt figured out, so I know the pains and joys of living in one of those much maligned red states, where the Bible verses flow as freely as the liquor we consume to make us all forget how fucked up everything really is. If you share my fate, sometimes it feels like making fun and drinking heavily are your only choices—and really, what two choices go better together?—but the recent election of Barack Obama shows that it's not time to give up hope yet. Not that you shouldn't drink or make fun of your moronic, often racist fellow state citizens, but you should do it with hope in your heart.

Because the 2008 election, if you'll recall, was much like the night you discovered multiple orgasms. One so-called red state after another fell to Obama, and every time, it was like, "Another one? *Wow!*" Virginia! North Carolina! Florida! Indiana! States that are known for being less than racially enlightened were voting not just for a Democrat, but for a black man, for president. Surely I wasn't the only one who woke up the next day and drank ten cups of coffee to convince myself that, yep, what I believed had happened the night before really had.

Political scientists will be sorting for years through the reasons why so many red states came around to the blue side, but for our purposes, just remember that few places are hopeless. And you can do a lot to help, mostly by investing in your community at home. One of the major forces that helps pull a red state blue is growing urban areas with distinctly liberal bents. Moving to one of those and simply being out and about helps. But if you can, do things for the community that help make it an attractive place for other smart, liberal people to move to. Art shows, music shows, anything "cultural," tend to be useful. An awesome coffee shop can make relocating more desirable for some people. Funky bars where interesting people congregate, and interesting restaurants with vegetarian options, make liberal types feel welcome. Make the stereotypes of yuppie liberals work for you! Push for public transportation, good schools, and nice parks.

Most of the old people around you have hardened into right-wing assholes. Accept this, and think outside the box when you're arguing with relatives about turning your red state blue. The politically active, nonpedantic person can be a huge asset to a social group full of well-meaning but largely apolitical people in convincing them to get a little more involved. Even if you're just nudging your friends toward remembering to vote or toward giving money to political campaigns, that helps.

Of course, you could always join the Democrats in your area and valiantly devote your time and energy to running candidates who will lose by smaller and smaller margins, until one day they hopefully tip the scales. This is incredibly useful work, and hats off to those who do it. But for those of us who don't have their emotional fortitude, there are other ways we can lay the groundwork to create communities that pull the United States toward the left.

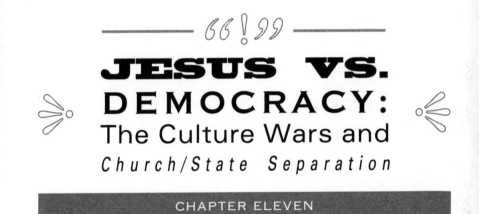

JESUS VS. DEMOCRACY:
The Culture Wars and
Church/State Separation

CHAPTER ELEVEN

GETTING TEENAGERS
Pregnant for God:
Abstinence-Only Education

If you want a window into the conflict between right-wing culture warriors and the rest of the country, you couldn't find one with more clarity than the issue of abstinence-only education. The controversy over sex education in the United States encapsulates everything you need to know about the right wing's behavior in the culture war: its sense of being victimized because it can't force its religion on everyone else, its dishonesty about its motives, its misogyny, and its sadism. Once you've peered into the heart of darkness and immersed yourself in the particulars of the debate, you will walk away with a really good idea of what makes social conservatism tick, which is useful for fighting back but will cause you many a sleepless night. In the interest of proving the explanatory power of the abstinence-only debate, I'll take on its components one at a time.

DISHONESTY

One of the fundamental things to understand about culture warriors is that they firmly believe that lying is an acceptable tactic in their balls-out war against the majority of Americans and our morally decrepit ways. The warriors' end, to remake America into a country full of people whose godliness is demonstrated by their misery, justifies their means: all sorts of lying, cheating, and violence. With abstinence-only education, the lying goes both inward and outward. Proponents lie both to the students within the program and to the adults outside who have the power to make it all stop once they find out what's really going on.

The favorite internal lie to the students is that condoms simply don't work (many reading materials cite a 30–50 percent failure rate, as if the authors didn't think that people who are already using condoms wouldn't notice it if we were getting pregnant every other year), though that's far from the only whopper the conservatives drop. Abstinence-only materials also state that having premarital sex will cause suicide and depression, and they're big on telling students, girls especially, that having premarital sex makes you too numb to love others or ever be loved again. Plausible but immoral lies, like "Condoms have tiny holes that HIV slips through," live right next to completely implausible lies, like "No two virgins who married have ever gotten divorced." It's hard to say if the implausible lies are included to make the plausible ones sound better by comparison, or if right-wingers are so truth-challenged that they can't tell the difference between a good lie and a transparent one.

The outward lie seems less lielike because it's a tad more complicated. Abstinence-only proponents know that it's illegal to use public schools for proselytizing, and that the whole argument for including sex education in the schools' curricula is that it's good for public-health outcomes. So the proponents push abstinence-only as if it were intended primarily as a public-health program to reduce unintended pregnancy and STD rates. This frame turns from being just a spin to being outright lying, however, when research demonstrates, as it has time and time again, that abstinence-only improves on comprehensive sex education regarding health outcomes in the same way the *Matrix* sequels improved on the original. Faced with evidence contradicting health-outcome claims, abstinence-only proponents will not stop declaring abstinence-only superior, and one has to conclude that they never cared about health outcomes in the first place. Telling teenagers not to fuck is its own reward, and any means necessary to defend that particular pleasure will be taken.

SADISM

The biggest lie culture warriors tell is that they care about you and want to help. Sadism motivates the hardcore warriors more than anything, and occasionally you see stark glimpses of it, such as when Republican state senator Dave Schultheis, of Colorado, said that he intended to vote against a bill requiring HIV tests for pregnant women, because he feared that having a chance of surviving longer with AIDS would be insufficient punishment for women who had sex. That kind of bold sadism doesn't tend to sell well with the general public, so culture warriors try to bury it, but in abstinence-only, you really see this type of loathing come out, this time aimed at young people with high hormone levels.

Abstinence-only allows a warrior to indulge sadism on both a direct and an indirect level. On the direct level, you get to shame a roomful of kids about having sexual desires, perhaps even singling out individual kids to bring to the front of the class for humiliation. You get to compare women who've had sex to used toothbrushes and chewed gum right to their faces. (After all, half the high school kids subjected to this abuse are already having sex.)

Many abstinence-only instructors also find creative ways to up their presentations' sadistic potential. Some illustrate the dangers of sex by ripping tape off students' arms or dangling bricks over students' genitals. Most alarmingly, though, one abstinence-only presenter in Ohio combines shaming kids about sex with his clown act, which involves hokey magic tricks in a frenzy of bad taste that might actually present a direct health hazard to the students he's torturing by making them watch.

Indirect sadism leads to scarier outcomes. The culture warriors' heavy emphasis on discouraging kids from using contraception moves quickly from their trying to trick kids into abstaining from sex right into their trying to punish kids who do have sex by introducing them to the territory of STDs and unintended pregnancy. The right wing's overjoyed responses to Sarah Palin's daughter Bristol's teenage pregnancy exposed this sadism very neatly: The girl fucked, and she paid for it by giving up her chance at a college career. In fact, the emphasis on demonizing contraception leads some people (okay, I'm in that group) to suggest that sadistically punishing people who have sex is the real point of abstinence-only, and encouraging abstinence is actually the secondary goal.

A great deal of abstinence-only "educational" writing dwells on fantasies about the various horrible punishments meted out by nature and god, often so baroque that it's impossible for all but the stupidest kids to take them at all seriously. The Texas Freedom Network released a report in 2009 reviewing various Texas abstinence-only materials and found a smorgasbord of examples in which "warning kids about the dangers of sex" skipped straight to "wishing all sorts of ill fates on kids" without passing Go to collect $200. Men who have sex before marriage and then marry will, according to one book, leave their wife almost certainly with "a radical hysterectomy, cervical cancer, and possibly death." Another brochure decided to go with the all-caps method to wish this upon kids: "FOR OUR YOUNG PEOPLE TO ENGAGE IN SEX NOW IS LIKE PLAYING RUSSIAN ROULETTE

WITH ALL BUT ONE CHAMBER FULL!" The entire adult population of fornicators has managed to survive without losing five-sixths of itself, but you can tell that the abstinence-only writers wish it wasn't so.

MISOGYNY AND HOMOPHOBIA

The theme of many abstinence-only materials could best be described as, "If gays could marry, who would get to be the husband?" Next to teaching kids that adults hate them and want them to die of AIDS, the next-most-important lesson abstinence-only pushes is that women are sucky crybabies and men are soulless bastards. The Texas Freedom Network found that the popular Why kNOw? curriculum states, "Women gauge their happiness and judge their success by their relationships," but for men, "happiness and success hinge on their accomplishments."

If you actually relied on abstinence-only materials to teach you about gender and sexual orientation, you'd find that gay people are just fooling themselves and are suicidal anyway, that straight men cannot contain themselves around women who wear miniskirts or even just snug T-shirts, and that women have very little interest in sex but enjoy weeping a lot while watching chick flicks.

The blogger Stacia L. Brown found a good example of this trend in pro-abstinence church programs that exploited the popularity of Beyoncé's song "Single Ladies (Put a Ring on It)." The song treads in the same sexist territory as a lot of pop music, suggesting that marriage is a tense exchange between a man who wants hot sex and a woman who provides it and wants payment in the form of a wedding ring. But the song makes no sense unless you assume the subject of it sampled the goods that he didn't put a ring on: "Don't be mad once you see that he want it / If you liked it then you shoulda put a ring on it." This song became a rallying cry for many in the "wait for marriage" crowd, despite this glaring inconsistency, probably because the sexism of the message spoke louder than casual acceptance of premarital sex.

PARANOID RELIGIOUS-PERSECUTION COMPLEX

Let's face it: People who think abstinence-only is a great idea tend to be the same people who send email forwards around about how the evil liberals are going to take "In God We Trust" off U.S. currency, thereby plunging our entire society into a godless hell where people fuck in the streets. (Hell, because it would suck to be pointedly not invited to the street orgies, a real risk when you're an asshole fundie.) You know, the same people who have been bitter for over four decades because of *Engel v. Vitale,* the Supreme Court decision banning school-mandated prayer. Ever since that fateful day in 1962, culture warriors have tried ever more elaborate methods to trick schools into declaring Christianity the super-bestest only real religion ever, the official-without-saying-so state religion.

Abstinence-only is just another form of smuggling religious materials into the classroom. If its proponents can't teach you that god says he made women out of men's ribs, then they're going to tell you to quit fucking and merely imply that god said so. In fact, many materials were originally Sunday-school books and pamphlets, which have been made "secular" with a halfhearted scrubbing that manages only to catch *some* of the Bible verses and descriptions of what god wants you to do with the dirty body parts he probably shouldn't have created in the first place.

The aforementioned Texas Freedom Network report found that classroom-provided abstinence-only materials had lots of "Oops, 'forgot' to scrub that" parts. Some materials told kids to marry only Christians, some had Bible verses throughout, and one compared being impregnated to being filled by the Holy Spirit. (Just in case you had any doubt that fundamentalist Christian men think that ejaculation is nothing short of a superpower.) I'm sure for the fundies pushing this stuff, it feels like an exciting form of resistance, but it's not the cool, pro-freedom resistance—it's more like the former high school football star who is still trying to tell himself that he's the man who pushes the nerds around, even as he has to ring up their purchases at the local convenience store.

One does wonder what the abstinence-only advocates hope to accomplish by slipping in these religious messages. Do they believe kids will think, *You know, fucking sounded like a waste of time anyway, and what's this? What are these "Bible" verses? If they have something to do with not fucking, then I'm onboard"?*

If abstinence-only comes up as an issue in your community, just remember this: The people who love this idea are the same people who are obsessed with the "problem" of declining birthrates in America, as well as with the "problem" of women who get educated and compete with men toe to toe in the workforce. If in fact abstinence-only managed to cause the teenage birthrate to skyrocket and women's college enrollment to decline, they'd probably be perfectly fine with that result.

TITHING HAS NOTHING ON THE
Government Teat: Faith-Based Funding

The Bush administration routinely committed atrocities against both common sense and common decency, and after a point, liberals resigned themselves to merely documenting the atrocities and saving their energy to protest only on those rare occasions when they thought they had a small chance of changing things, or when it was so important (such as with the Iraq War) that even futile protest seemed necessary for posterity's sake. Liberals let a lot of stuff slide, and faith-based funding led the pack—despite the fact that to think it's even remotely okay, people have to have tremendous disdain for the basic separation of church and state.

To refresh your memory: The First Amendment to the Constitution clearly states that the state cannot establish religion. The courts have interpreted this consistently as the states' showing neutrality on the subject of religious dogma, i.e., staying completely out of the superiority wars between various religions and denominations. It's so indefensible to give some groups money *because* they're religiously affiliated over other groups offering the same services that I wouldn't be surprised if some desperate defender of faith-based funding tried, for shits and giggles, to argue that giving people money couldn't be construed as showing them favor. Much was written about the uses and abuses of faith-based funding under the Bush administration, but since the Bush administration benefited so handsomely from such a wide, unchecked giveaway to the religious right, it felt pointless to pick a major fight over it. Surely the next Democrat in office would flick away those abuses as it implemented other obvious policy reversals, such as shutting down the global gag rule, right?

Hopefully we've learned our lesson about taking for granted even those things any moron should take for granted. The resistance to faith-based funding was slight, and as soon as Obama got into office, instead of reversing the Bush-era executive decision to funnel money to churches (which probably already have plenty, if they can afford to lobby for it), he set up an initiative to continue handing tax money directly to religious organizations, calling the initiative the Office of Faith-Based and Neighborhood Partnerships. But it's been difficult for liberals to gain the momentum to protest this decision, because we figure Obama's one of our guys, and so he's somehow doing this "right." Indeed, he's probably not as quick to just write big checks to fundamentalist Christians who hope the world will end soon, but that's somewhat like giving your current boyfriend a pass for leaving dirty condoms on your pillow because your last boyfriend took a shit on your porch.

One of the Bush administration's main objectives, to be blunt, was to shore up the Republican base by giving a bunch of evangelical organizations a ton of money, so the administration could increase "Jeebus, gay marriage, abortion" panic to the point where no one would even remember that they shouldn't vote for Republicans if they liked having a secure job that paid their bills. The more government money the administration secured to start programs, the more people it could hire, and the more it grew. Outside of just faith-based funding for community service projects, there was also an enormous amount of abstinence-only funding that ended up in evangelical pockets because the evangelists just so happened to be the ones printing the textbooks necessary to waste kids' time after they were told to quit fucking.

Faith-based funding also appeals to what many conservative Christians treat as their main, and quite possibly only, issue—being considered the best and most important people in the country. Most of their issues, from abortion (make our dogma law!) to school prayer (believers above nonbelievers in classrooms, boo-yah!) to the war on terror (interpreted as a religious war that'll prove that they're better than Muslims once and for all), reflect this single-minded mission.

The Obama administration has indicated that it intends to do the faith-based thing but do it the right way, without making it a right-wing, Christian gravy train. Just like I fully intend to buy coffee creamer before it runs out, but then I once again find myself cursing the very existence of caffeine, coffee cups, and mornings. Somehow, we human beings fail when we set such lofty expectations for ourselves. Obama justified continuing the program by stating that under his administration, the groups wouldn't be allowed to use government money to proselytize or discriminate in their hiring against gays or nonbelievers.

The hope that the government could tap that vein of good Christians who practice tolerance and also have no problem with breaking down the separation of church and state turned out to be short-lived. After Obama put together the Council on Faith-Based and Neighborhood Partnerships, Sarah Posner of the American Prospect discovered that most of the members were men and all but two (who were Jewish) supported banning abortion. Fundamentalist Christians had spent years working on convincing the country that Christianity was more about keeping the ladies in the kitchen than about achieving peace on Earth, and the Obama administration decided to roll right over for them.

Grouchy atheists like me pointed out that this sort of thing was inevitable. If you're a pro-science, pro-choice, pro-gay liberal, being a Christian seems somewhat beside the point. You can be all those things and be an atheist, which means that you can use your Saturday nights to do the sorts of things that evangelicals think will bring Jesus's judgment on this country and know that you can sleep until noon the next day. Airtight logic like this is why "nonbeliever" is the fastest-growing religious category in the country.

But if you're some uptight straight dude who wants women in the kitchen and gays in the closet, then you need religion, because you can constantly foist responsibility for your own dickitude onto god.

Not that there aren't religious liberals who could use those positions of power and that stream of cash into their coffers. But they can't beat the system, even when they have a fellow liberal Christian in office calling the shots. They'll never win the whining-and-leg-kicking contest necessary to get hold of those offices and cash. Right-wing Christians will always be able to pull the "not a real Christian" card more effectively on their brethren, in part because they're bigger babies who make more noise, and in part because everyone else has to concede that atheists have a point about the advisability of sleeping in on Sunday if your politics are indistinguishable from your nonbelieving liberal friends'.

You can almost put yourself in Obama's shoes—what's the point of putting people on a faith-based anything when they look and act exactly like a bunch of secular people who give their money to the ACLU instead of tithing it at church? He didn't start off seeing it that way, but spend enough time around kicking, whining, screaming right-wing nuts, and suddenly it just seems easier to give in to their demands. Especially since the damn office only existed in the first place as a way to funnel money to the whiners who feel left out of a modern America where women work for a living, people have sex for fun, and the art of sleeping in on Sunday mornings helps keep the bars flush with cash on Saturday night.

THIS PLACE SUCKS,
and We Want a Rapture

I'm sure that diligent sociologists around the world have devoted years of research to trying to figure out the meteoric rise of the religious right, and all the social factors that have gone into it. I'm sure that you will want to read that research in other books. But in this purely unscientific chapter, I'm going to argue that it's surprisingly simple—the religious right has really honed its appeal to life's losers by making the dual promise that it's going to punish others on their behalf, and that it's the losers' ticket out of this filthy shithole of a life. Worse, now that the right is a couple of generations in, it's really figured out how to keep the racket going by creating a constantly replenishing supply of young people whom it prohibits from enjoying the pleasures of modern secular society and who will happily judge and punish those who aren't so unfortunate.

If you doubt this simplistic reading of the situation, I highly recommend hanging out at an anti-abortion protest, but remember to wear your potato sack, ladies, because you really don't want the scruffy middle-aged guys who populate these things to gawk at you. Enjoy the smorgasbord of bitterness from men unable to charm a lady into cleaning up after them, men who've convinced themselves that if birth control and abortion were illegal, they would have had at least one shot at nailing someone down to financial dependence, even if it took a massive amount of liquor to make that happen.

It's generally frowned upon in our discourse to dismiss our political enemies by claiming that they're losers, but mostly because it's a tactic used in entirely inappropriate situations. For instance, anti-feminists like to claim feminists exist only because they're unfuckable losers, but this has never made much sense. Feminists wouldn't have a whole lot of motivation to push for reproductive rights and against intimate violence if we as a group had no personal need for these things. But let's face it: The religious right's entire mentality doesn't make sense unless its followers just generally hate life and want to punish and escape.

Take the group's organizing fantasy: the Rapture. For people who go out of their way to call themselves professing Christians, it's more than a little telling that they cling to a belief in it, a belief that has no real basis in the Bible. Oh, sure, they claim the basis is there, but only through a series of stretched interpretations that are so flexible, they could be used to claim the Bible outlaws playing Super Mario Brothers. In reality, the Rapture is a folk belief that really got its claws in the population after it became the basis for a series of horribly written pulp novels called the *Left Behind* series. The books provide the red-meat fantasy to believers.

Even the movie *Revenge of the Nerds* had more subtlety as a revenge fantasy than the Rapture does. For my readers unaware of what the Rapture is all about, it's pretty simple. Its proponents believe that one day, god's going to decide that he's tired of this TV show called *Life on Earth* and wants to cancel it. But, since he's god, he can't do it quietly. No, he's going to start off by yanking all the Bible-believing losers up into heaven, and then he's going to turn the planet into hell on Earth, where the ugliest war of all time will be fought against the Antichrist while the true believers sit cackling in heaven, saying, "Ha ha! You thought you were cute, with your sex and your senses of humor and your book learning and your ability to scratch some joy out of this mortal coil. Well, who's laughing now, fuckers?" And you can say "fuckers" in heaven, because God can't unrapture the raptured. That would create a crack in the space-time continuum that would keep Marty McFly from ever being born, as you are no doubt aware.

Losers who get through life subsisting on childish fantasies of revenge seem like they wouldn't be a big enough group to really swing elections or wholly own an American political party, but, sadly, this is where we're at nowadays. How did things get to the point where we could populate entire nations with our embittered losers with childish fantasies?

Many culprits come to mind, not the least being the TV set, which portrays most of the population as if it's living in a bubble where everyone's upper middle class and has an exciting sex life, the sort of thing that could really make a person bitter if you were slow-witted enough to believe it's true. But there are so many more villains. Our shitty education system no doubt shares the blame, especially when it comes to creating people so slow-witted that TV has this much sway over them. Old-fashioned American anti-intellectualism has a role to play.

But the biggest demons chewing people down to loser size are our overwork and isolation. We're gradually being crafted into the perfect worker bees for corporate America—no distracting social lives, stunted interior lives that reduce the possibility of rebellion, and ever-shrinking amounts of free time being gobbled up by work obligations. Loneliness and boredom have become the rule of the land, and a constantly growing number of people are cracking under the pressure and drifting from being just lonely people who need to get out a little more into utter loserdom—and that's when the right wing pounces.

Like any intelligent social movement, however, the right has an eye toward growth and sustaining itself into the future. With that in mind, it's doing everything in its power to stoke the fires that create the losers. Don't think that deliberate inculcation of sexual ignorance is strictly ideological! If you can deliberately manufacture a population that's aching with a bunch of desires it can barely articulate, and then produce people to hate who are happy fuckers, hate it will.

Ignorance is the other key component of the right wing's mission. Ignorance breeds stupidity, and stupid people are easy to stoke resentment in, because they feel the world is passing them by, as all these people keep talking about stuff they just don't understand. To this end, the religious right injects in them creationism, anti-science attitudes, and beliefs about how knowing the truth about history makes them traitors to their country. If it can, it also tries to scare them off having too much interaction with the real world. That's the whole function of Christian rock, for instance—by aping sounds that are a mere twenty years out of date, Christian rockers can make the young feel like they have enough fun that they don't need to get out much.

Once the religious right has its new crop of fundies—undersexed, undereducated, and scared of the world outside—then it's a quick jump to more fantasies of the Rapture, and it's got more immediate political energy to use to punish the people who aren't crippled by being losers.

PRAYING AT SCHOOL:
The Cheapest Status Symbol

The religious right pulls as heavily as it does from America's loser population in no small part by feeding them a story about how they're entitled. The story goes like this: This country was founded by people like us—good, wholesome Christians—*for* people like us. All those parts of the Constitution outlining rights were written in a time when it never even occurred to the founding fathers that the writing could be understood to mean that women could have abortions and even non-Christian religions could exist in the United States, or, worse, that people without religion could be allowed to exist at all. But now the country's been hijacked by a bunch of liberals who want to turn it into a hellhole of the sort of freedoms that the founders never intended when they said that people should be free. And it's our duty to reclaim the country for ourselves, the true inheritors of the founders' vision.

It's an incoherent fairy tale. After all, few people who tell this tale want to restore the nation to what it was in 1789, when slavery was legal and women couldn't vote. (Nor will they admit that the founders most definitely didn't want a "Christian nation," but really did intend for religious freedom to exist, when they enshrined it in the First Amendment.) The process of changing the country from what it was in revolutionary times to the one it is now was a gradual process, but every wingnut has his own idea about when the nation really went off the deep end. In fact, you can generally tell what kind of wingnut you're working with based on this question. The more genteel, economic wingnuts think the country's been going to hell ever since FDR averted a socialist revolution by passing the New Deal, instead of the preferred method of creating a lottery wherein once a week, the unlucky working-class person who drew the wrong lot was shot until all talk of socialism, communism, labor unions, or labor reform was ended. But for social conservatives, especially the religious right, things went off the rails in the 1950s, or when *Leave It to Beaver* went off the air. (The difference between TV and reality is weak in this sector of society.) Or, for political purposes, the country officially went to hell in 1962, when the Supreme Court decided *Engel v. Vitale,* which banned school prayer.

You can't single out one Supreme Court decision from the string of right-wing irritants that the court issued in the 1950s through the '70s. Schools were desegregated, birth control and abortion were legalized, and even private schools were told they couldn't segregate. But people do forget how school prayer topped the list of judicial infractions, because it struck right at the heart of the most important of all religious-right beliefs: that this country rightfully belongs to it, and everyone else who lives here must pay tribute to its superiority.

Because of all the belligerent whining about how America is a "Christian nation," there can be no doubt that school prayer is about establishing a hierarchy of Real Americans who are better than the hodgepodge of non-Christians and nonbelievers. From fundies' perspective, the demands to keep officially "nondenominational" (albeit obviously Christian) prayer out of schools constitutes a huge overreach by lesser Americans. They give us the right to vote and live in relative peace, so why can't we honor their superiority to us by making our kids mouth their prayers?

Failure to ritually recognize Christianity as a prerequisite for being a Real American is singled out as a major precursor to all the other going-to-hell signposts. Kids quit genuflecting to the superiority of Christians, and next thing you know, women think they can sex without having babies, gays think they can go out in public and even get married, and someone who wasn't even a Republican got a blow job in the White House!

Because of this belief, the religious right puts a great deal of effort and money into denying that the founding fathers wished for a separation of church and state and instead argue that we can have just a little bit of theocracy here and there. Just a little acknowledgment that the fundies are better than everyone else can't really hurt, can it? They'll just slip it in a little, but they promise that you won't wake up in the morning rolling in theocratic splooge.

Call it the "a little theocracy goes a long way" movement. It nibbles around the edges of church-and-state separation. It tries to get its religious beliefs into the science classroom under the guise of "teaching the controversy." If the right can't have teacher-led prayer, it'll have student-led prayer that's supposed to be nondenominational, but the right can't help it if the kid in charge doesn't know how to pray in a way that's not evangelical. A little bit of faith-based funding couldn't hurt, either, even if that's an objective instance of the government's paying religious groups directly. And here, the right can slip in a little censorship of concepts that offend its religious sensibilities, and call it "community standards." And let's restrict abortion while we're at it, because while the right objects to it for religious reasons, it can distract you from those reasons by bombarding you with graphic descriptions of the surgery.

The half-measures thing doesn't make sense if the members of the religious right honestly believe that the United States had to be an officially Christian nation to make good with god. But it makes perfect sense if they see the glimpses of the church in the state as a pat on the back for themselves, as a small reminder to lesser Americans that the fundies are the ones who get little hat-tips. Sure, the bigger the tip, the better, but the important thing is getting it in the first place. Which is why this battle will always be fought on the edges, over the minutia—or at least it will be as long as we still have an official separation of church and state.

PROMOTING
A SECULAR SOCIETY
Isn't Anti-Religion

—— 66 ! 99 ——

God knows I wish it were, since I'm an unrepentant atheist who dreads going to church, for fear that I won't be able to contain my squeals of laughter every time someone says something I consider ridiculous. (Last time I had to occupy a spot in a pew, I wished fervently that I could figure out how to use Twitter on my iPhone discreetly, so powerful was my urge to make droll comments about the goings-on.) I wish we had a way to just wipe religion out so that people who spend their time and money on church could instead devote it to more useful outlets, such as charity and sleeping in on Sunday.

But the truth is that religious people have as much cause to demand a secular government and public life as the hellbound nonbelievers do. No matter how much the people who revolt against the secularism laid out in the Constitution may try to talk blandly of "people of faith"— as if they can make general statements about what "of faith" agrees with that dirty atheists don't—the truth is that everyone pushing for more religion in government is working an angle, an angle called "my magical beliefs are better than yours." So, no matter how much you value your faith, you should want it protected from government intrusions pushed by those who'd like to break down the divider between church and state.

So I beg of you, religious readers, to take up the cause of secularism with as much ardor as atheists do. We don't have to agree that there's a god or gods to agree that the right-wing crazies who think the Bible is mostly a screed against gays and abortion don't need to be telling us whose religious dogma should dictate the laws of the land. Don't call out the religious right only as people who are mistaken in their attitudes toward gays, women, or whoever else they have in their sights; also call them out for their disregard of the First Amendment mandate for separation of church and state.

It means more coming from you religious people. The public at large thinks atheists who push for a secular society are just assholes who are trying to get out of going to church to make our moms happy. But if religious people speak up about the benefits of secular society—in which they get to practice their religion in peace, free from concerns about the law's dictating dogma they don't share—then suddenly it's much harder to dismiss secularists. Admit it, religious peo-

ABOUT
the Author

© MARC FALETTI

Amanda Marcotte writes about politics and feminism for the blog Pandagon.net, as well as for other outlets, such as RH Reality Check, *The American Prospect,* the *Guardian* (U.K.), *Salon,* AOL, and the *Los Angeles Times.* She lives for breakfast tacos, cheap vinyl records, improving her guitar playing in the video game Rock Band, and not letting her bitterness over *Bush v. Gore* get her down. She loves writing books and creating multimedia, including a fortunate/unfortunate stint playing Sarah Palin on YouTube. She lives in Austin, Texas, with her two cats, her boyfriend, and her collection of Devo kitsch.

ACKNOWLEDGMENTS

To Jesse Taylor, Pam Spaulding, Brandon Thornburg, and everyone who's done time at Pandagon: You are my heroes, and I hope we have many years together kicking ass and taking names, wingnut names. Thanks, as always, to Brooke Warner and Jessica Valenti for looking at me and thinking, *Sure, she could write a book.* Thanks to the entire staff at RH Reality Check for their enthusiasm and their willingness to get what it takes to make it in this brave new multimedia world.

Friends who listen to my political ramblings, thank you. Lindsay Beyerstein and Darcy James Argue, you guys are true friends I shall always be grateful for. Thanks to Lindsay twice for always being patient with even my weirdest requests. Shout-out to Diana Gerson for being a lot of fun, but also for reminding me that going out and doing this work does mean something at the end of the day. Thanks to Samhita Mukhopadhyay for always challenging me to be a savvier, better version of myself, and thanks also for the biggest laugh I had at South by Southwest. Kiki Powell, thanks for being the one friend who cares nothing for this world of mine and probably won't even read these acknowledgments. I need the break that hanging out with you gives me. Thanks for the space, Michael Spinetta. And thanks to the Spiderhouse for giving me the perfect place to write while consuming unhealthy amounts of breakfast tacos.

Thank you to Marc Faletti. You wrestle over ideas with me, assume I'm imperfect and don't care, and have always, always believed in me, even when I've been skeptical. I'm so glad that you looked out into the wide world and found me.

SELECTED TITLES FROM SEAL PRESS

For more than thirty years, Seal Press has published groundbreaking books. By women. For women. Visit our website at www.sealpress.com. Check out the Seal Press blog at www.sealpress.com/blog.

It's a Jungle Out There: The Feminist Survival Guide to Politically Inhospitable Environments, by Amanda Marcotte. $13.95, 978-1-58005-226-9. All the witty comebacks, in-your-face retorts, and priceless advice women need to survive in politically hostile environments.

Full Frontal Feminism: A Young Woman's Guide to Why Feminism Matters, by Jessica Valenti. $15.95, 978-1-58005-201-6. A sassy and in-your-face look at contemporary feminism for women of all ages.

Click: Young Women on the Moments That Made Them Feminists, edited by Courtney E. Martin and J. Courtney Sullivan. $16.95, 978-1-58005-285-6. Notable writers and celebrities entertain and illuminate with true stories recalling the distinct moments when they knew they were feminists.

Girldrive: Criss-Crossing America, Redefining Feminism, by Nona Willis Aronowitz and Emma Bee Bernstein. $19.95, 978-1-58005-273-3. Two young women set out on the open road to explore the current state of feminism in the United States.

He's A Stud, She's A Slut, and 49 Other Double Standards Every Woman Should Know, by Jessica Valenti. $13.95, 978-1-58005-245-0. With sass, humor, and aplomb, *Full Frontal Feminism* author Jessica Valenti takes on the obnoxious double standards women encounter every day.

Listen Up: Voices from the Next Feminist Generation, edited by Barbara Findlen. $16.95, 978-1-58005-054-8. A collection of essays featuring the voices of today's young feminists on racism, sexuality, identity, AIDS, revolution, abortion, and much more.